T0419698

WILDLIFE PROTECTION, DESTRUCTION AND EXTINCTION SERIES

CONSERVATION RESEARCH IN UGANDA'S FORESTS: A REVIEW OF SITE HISTORY, RESEARCH, AND USE OF RESEARCH IN UGANDA'S FOREST PARKS AND BUDONGO FOREST RESERVE

WILDLIFE PROTECTION, DESTRUCTION AND EXTINCTION SERIES

International Illegal Trade in Wildlife
Liana Sun Wyler and Pervaze A. Sheikh
2008. ISBN: 978-1-60456-757-1

National Parks and Rivers: Background, Protection and Use Issues
Yolanda A. Reddy (Editor)
2009. ISBN: 978-1-60741-801-6

Wildlife: Destruction, Conservation and Biodiversity
John D. Harris and Paul L. Brown (Editors)
2009. ISBN: 978-1-60692-974-2

Wildlife Refuges: Factors and Concerns about Future Sustainability
Earl B. Taylor (Editor)
2010. ISBN: 978-1-60692-683-3

Conservation Research in Uganda's Forests: A Review of Site History, Research, and Use of Research in Uganda's Forest Parks and Budongo Forest Reserve
William Olupot and Andrew J. Plumptre
2010. ISBN: 978-1-60876-577-5

WILDLIFE PROTECTION, DESTRUCTION AND EXTINCTION SERIES

CONSERVATION RESEARCH IN UGANDA'S FORESTS: A REVIEW OF SITE HISTORY, RESEARCH, AND USE OF RESEARCH IN UGANDA'S FOREST PARKS AND BUDONGO FOREST RESERVE

WILLIAM OLUPOT

AND

ANDREW J. PLUMPTRE

Nova Science Publishers, Inc.

New York

NOTICE TO THE READER

The Publisher has taken reasonable care in the preparation of this book, but makes no expressed or implied warranty of any kind and assumes no responsibility for any errors or omissions. No liability is assumed for incidental or consequential damages in connection with or arising out of information contained in this book. The Publisher shall not be liable for any special, consequential, or exemplary damages resulting, in whole or in part, from the readers' use of, or reliance upon, this material.

Independent verification should be sought for any data, advice or recommendations contained in this book. In addition, no responsibility is assumed by the publisher for any injury and/or damage to persons or property arising from any methods, products, instructions, ideas or otherwise contained in this publication.

This publication is designed to provide accurate and authoritative information with regard to the subject matter covered herein. It is sold with the clear understanding that the Publisher is not engaged in rendering legal or any other professional services. If legal or any other expert assistance is required, the services of a competent person should be sought. FROM A DECLARATION OF PARTICIPANTS JOINTLY ADOPTED BY A COMMITTEE OF THE AMERICAN BAR ASSOCIATION AND A COMMITTEE OF PUBLISHERS.

LIBRARY OF CONGRESS CATALOGING-IN-PUBLICATION DATA
Olupot, William.
  Conservation research in Uganda's forests : a review of site history, research, and use of research in Uganda's forest parks and Budongo Forest Reserve / William Olupot.
    p. cm.
  Includes bibliographical references and index.
  ISBN 978-1-60876-577-5 (hardcover : alk. paper)
  1. Forests and forestry--Research--Uganda. 2. Forest conservation--Uganda. 3. National parks and reserves--Uganda. I. Title.
  SD356.54.U33O48 2009
  333.75096761--dc22
                        2009041937

Published by Nova Science Publishers, Inc. ✦ New York

CONTENTS

PREFACE

In recent decades, there has been increased interest in understanding ecosystems in order to be able to manage and conserve them. Yet examples of how research directly supports conservation are rare. Protected area managers and policy makers need scientific information from protected areas for policy development and to effectively devise, revise, and implement management strategies. Researchers seek a clear understanding of what types of research can directly support conservation efforts to guide them in the design of such projects. A variety of perspectives of what constitutes 'conservation' or 'applied' wildlife research may exist, and indeed conservation priorities do differ between sites so that ultimately, what we describe here is from one perspective and designing projects that directly support site conservation depends on a prior understanding of issues at the site. This book is intended to encourage thinking about what constitutes conservation research to be able to better develop projects that directly support conservation. The aim of this book is to encourage research that directly benefits conservation in protected areas by reviewing applied research and providing examples in which it has been used for conservation purposes.

FORWARD

Richard Wrangham

Peabody Museum, Harvard University, Cambridge, MA 02138, USA
Kibale Chimpanzee Project, Fort Portal, Uganda

Tropical forests are the major storehouse of the world's biodiversity. Sixty million years ago they covered most of the world's land surface. Cool dry climates now restrict them to equatorial latitudes. Since human foods tend to grow more easily in grasslands than in forests, the expansion of human populations has reduced them further. Add such pressures as commercial exploitation of trees for wood or charcoal, the hunting of animals and competition from invasive plants, and the result is clear. Tropical forests are in trouble. Worldwide surveys of their future tend to foresee them dwindling to near zero area by the end of the 21st century. We risk losing the major part of life of earth, priceless genetic variation, a link to our past and unknown potential sources of practical and aesthetic value for our species.

While the global trends are pervasive, they are not uniform. Some forests risk wholesale cutting for large new agricultural projects. Some face death by a thousand cuts: the nibbles of individual families enlarging their fields, the one-by-one removal of logs for charcoal, the trampling of young growth by cattle. The consequences of the different pressures for biodiversity and environmental services vary even more, depending on the particular mix of species, water regimes, soil types and other ecological conditions. So each area of tropical forest contains its own special combination of biological and geographical importance, and each faces its own particular cascade of threats. The knowledge that is needed to counter threats, reverse negative trends and manage these invaluable forests must be local, detailed and specific.

That is why this book is so important. Uganda has an exceptional tradition of tropical forest research stretching back to the early part of the twentieth century, but much of the information is inaccessible, hidden in elusive reports. With decades of experience working in several different forests and for varied organizations, William Olupot and Andrew Plumptre have been able to extract jewels of data from diverse sources. As they remind us, knowledge is power. This book provides the knowledge that offers opportunities for improved management. It also shows where exciting research opportunities lie open.

Improved knowledge aids forest conservation by enlisting help. The level of relevant information is still generally poor. For instance nowhere in tropical forests, not even in Uganda, is there a good identification guide to all the major taxa of animals and plants. But the accounts that Olupot and Plumptre have assembled of the natural history of six forests provide an excellent base for such developments and thereby offer practical promise. The more species that people can identify in a given habitat, the more those people will identify emotionally with the place. The more stories that emerge of the biological peculiarities and biotic intricacies that tie a forest's life to place, the stronger the constituencies of people who can be expected to speak up for the value of these vital habitats.

I was privileged in 1991 to attend a meeting of the officers of Uganda's Forest Department which aimed to generate a longterm philosophy. The question at stake was whether the forests should be managed like an agricultural crop, weeding out "useless" trees like figs and turning the natural storehouses into restricted plantations of trees such as mahogany; or whether the future lay with taking advantage of the natural services provided by intact forests. For two days points and counter-points were presented with passion, but in a vote at the end the answer was unambiguous: it was for conservation.

This book is a tribute to that future.

ACKNOWLEDGMENTS

Preliminary versions of the manuscript were reviewed by Colin A. Chapman, John M. Kasenene, Gilbert Isabirye-Basuta, Bob Plumptre, Vernon Reynolds, Derek Pomeroy, and Peter M. Waser. We deeply appreciate their putting time into this. We would like to thank the managements of the Uganda Wildlife Authority and Makerere University Biological Field Station for allowing us unrestricted access to their libraries and Colin Chapman for permission to access his personal library. The review was funded by the Wildlife Conservation Society, the John D. and Catherine T. MacArthur Foundation and the Daniel K. Thorne Foundation.

LIST OF ACRONYMS AND SYNONYMS

ADF	Allied Democratic Front
BFP	Budongo Forest Project
BFR	Budongo Forest Reserve – Budongo (syn.)
BINP	Bwindi Impenetrable National Park – Bwindi (syn.)
CARE	Cooperative Assistance and Relief Everywhere
CFR	Central Forest Reserve
CI	Conservation International
CRM	Community Resource Management
DRC	Democratic Republic of Congo
GEF	Global Environmental Facility
FR	Forest Reserve
ICD	Integrated Conservation and Development
IFCP	Impenetrable Forest Conservation Project
ITFC	Institute of Tropical Forest Conservation
IUCN	International Union for the Conservation of Nature
KNP	Kibale National Park – Kibale (syn.)
KSDP	Kibale-Semliki Development Project
KVNP	Kidepo Valley National Park
LMNP	Lake Mburo National Park
MBIFCT	Mgahinga Bwindi Impenetrable Conservation Trust
MENP	Mt Elgon National Park – Mt Elgon (syn.)
MFNP	Murchison Falls National Park
MGNP	Mgahinga Gorilla National Park – Mgahinga (syn.)
MUBFS	Makerere University Biological Field Station
MUIENR	Makerere University Institute of Environment and Natural Resources
NFA	National Forest Authority

NGO	Non- Government Organization
NP	National Park
NRM	National Resistance Movement
NYZS	New York Zoological Society – now WCS
QENP	Queen Elizabeth National Park
RNP	Rwenzori National Park – Rwenzori (syn.)
SNP	Semliki National Park – Semliki (syn.)
UNESCO	United Nations Educational, Scientific, and Cultural Organization
UNP	Uganda National Parks
UPC	Uganda Peoples Congress
UWA	Uganda Wildlife Authority
WCI	Wildlife Conservation International – now WCS
WCS	Wildlife Conservation Society
WWF	World Wide Fund for Nature

ABOUT THE AUTHORS

William Olupot has been studying the behaviour and ecology of wildlife in Uganda for over 15 years. Initially focusing on primate behaviour in Kibale forest, he has worked in Bwindi, Mgahinga, Murchison Falls, and Queen Elizabeth National Parks and has a good knowledge of the ecology of all parks in Uganda. He studied at Purdue University to obtain his doctorate in primate ecology and dispersal. He has been a research specialist in the Wildlife Conservation Society's (WCS) Uganda Country Programme, focusing on diverse conservation topics such as edge effects, threats to species in human-dominated landscapes, and bushmeat socioeconomics. He is presently coordinating efforts to reduce unsustainable hunting of wildlife for bushmeat in Eastern Africa.

Andrew Plumptre has been working in east and central Africa for 20 years. He obtained his doctorate from Bristol University studying the ecology of large mammals in the Virunga Volcanoes. He then investigated the impacts of sustainable logging practices on wildlife in Uganda, in the Budongo Forest Reserve, before becoming the Assistant Director for the WCS's Africa Program in New York. In 2000 he returned to Uganda and and then established a programme for the Wildlife Conservation Society focusing on the conservation of the Albertine Rift. He is the author of over 100 publications on the ecology and conservation of this region.

Chapter 1

INTRODUCTION

In recent decades, there has been increased interest in understanding ecosystems in order to be able to manage and conserve them. Yet examples of how research directly supports conservation are rare. Protected area managers and policy makers need scientific information from protected areas for policy development and to effectively devise, revise, and implement management strategies. Researchers seek a clear understanding of what types of research can directly support conservation efforts to guide them in the design of such projects. A variety of perspectives of what constitutes 'conservation' or 'applied' wildlife research may exist, and indeed conservation priorities do differ between sites so that ultimately, what we describe here is from one perspective and designing projects that directly support site conservation depends on a prior understanding of issues at the site. This review is intended to encourage thinking about what constitutes conservation research to be able to better develop projects that directly support conservation. It gives high priority to research that informs protected area managers about how well conservation efforts are doing and that which points to specific actions that managers and conservation practitioners need to take to ensure biodiversity conservation. Emphasis is also made on research that supports or provides a basis for sustainable use of biological resources.

This review is based on research in Uganda's six forest parks: Bwindi Impenetrable National Park (BINP), Mgahinga Gorilla National Park (MGNP), Mt. Elgon National Park (MENP, Rwenzori Mountains National Park (RMNP), Kibale National Park (KNP), and Semliki National Park (SNP). We also review research from Budongo Forest Reserve (BFR). Some surveys and research have taken place in other forest reserves in the country, and so we also refer to them where relevant.

Uganda is one of the most biodiverse countries in Africa, containing more than half of Africa's bird species and a very diverse set of vegetation types from the montane flora at 5,000 metres in the Rwenzoris to the lowland forest at 600 metres in the Semliki valley. The natural forests of Uganda only form about 3% of the total vegetation cover in the country but contain a much higher percentage of this biodiversity (probably about 50-60%). As in many countries around the world, natural forest cover in Uganda is declining, falling from about 12.5% to less than 2% between 1900 and 1990 (Grove 1995). Rwenzori National Park, Mt Elgon National Park, Mgahinga Gorilla National Park, and Bwindi Impenetrable National Park are some of the 70 protected areas found in the Afromontane biogeographical unit. Along with Cape Fynbos in South Africa, Afromontane forest is the rarest vegetation type on the continent.

All the protected areas except for Mt Elgon NP lie within the western arm of the Great Rift Valley, an area of global importance for biodiversity conservation. The small remnant forests in this cluster extend from Mahale mountains National Park and Mt Kabobo north to the Rwenzori mountains (IUCN 1994b) and Budongo Forest Reserve. Popularly known as the Albertine Rift, this region is widely recognized by global conservation organizations. Conservation International has identified it as part of the Eastern Afromontane Biodiversity Hotspot meaning that it contains many endemic species and is highly threatened; WWF identifies this area as a Global 200 Ecoregion, and Birdlife International as an Endemic Bird Area.

These protected areas include a variety of land forms and plant communities, which provide habitats for a wide variety of wildlife. They are outstanding for the conservation of plant and vertebrate communities. In addition, the forests provide important ecological services, attracting and retaining rainfall and providing a slow release of water to the surrounding human-occupied areas, regulating the local climate, and providing forest products to many consumers in the country.

Despite these values, the conservation of these areas is complex, partly being a function of biological factors as the forests are generally small and largely isolated from one another; and partly a function of human factors. In small isolated forests, component species usually exist at low population levels, and, without nearby sources of replenishment, are at a high risk of extinction. In addition, south west Uganda and the area around Mt Elgon have some of the highest densities of people in Africa leading to acute pressures on the protected areas. The high density of people creates hard edges along the boundaries of gazetted forests. There has also been an over-exploitation of potentially renewable resources such as ungulate populations, valuable timber, and non-timber forest products such as rattan.

Most of the research in Uganda's forests has been carried out in Kibale under the auspices of Makerere University Biological Field Station (MUBFS), in Bwindi Impenetrable National Park (BINP) under the Institute of Tropical Forest Conservation (ITFC), and in Budongo Forest Reserve under the Budongo Forest Conservation Project (BFCP). Research in MUBFS started in 1970 when the Kibale Forest Project was established by Dr. Tom Struhsaker, a research Zoologist for WCI (Wildlife Conservation International of the New York Zoological Society, now Wildlife Conservation Society) who embarked on a study of the red colobus monkey at the Kanyawara site primarily but later studies of other species and issues expanded to the Ngogo site in the forest. His studies continued for 18 years. In March 1987, a contract between Makerere University and the New York Zoological Society was signed whereby the university would assume administration of the field station over a five-year period. Initially most of the research work in this forest focused on primates but this expanded to studies of the general ecology of the forest and the socioeconomic conditions faced by the local communities.

BFCP was established at the Sonso site in Budongo by Dr. Vernon Reynolds in 1990 to investigate the responses of wildlife to timber harvesting and to conserve the chimpanzee populations of the forest. Studies initially focused on the impact of logging on primate species. The research later broadened to include other faunal groups such as small mammals and birds. ITFC started as The Impenetrable Forest Conservation Project (IFCP) which was created after surveys of the forest in 1984 showed that Bwindi Impenetrable Forest Reserve was very valuable for conservation. Initiated by Dr. Tom Butynski in 1986 at Ruhija to support forest research and gorilla conservation, it focused initially on the gorilla population found in this forest and the biodiversity of the forest. The findings of these studies helped promote upgrading of the forest reserve to National Park and World Heritage Site status. ITFC was established in 1991 as a research facility of the Mbarara University of Science and Technology, replacing the IFCP. Since establishment of the three research stations, scientists from all the 5 continents have conducted studies in these institutions for masters, doctoral theses, post graduate projects, and long-term research programs. Kibale NP, Bwindi Impenetrable NP, and Budongo FR are thus the main source of the information we have on Ugandan forests today.

The aim of this book is to encourage research that directly benefits conservation by reviewing applied research and providing examples in which it has been used for conservation purposes. In preparing the review, we realize that there are always different perspectives of what constitutes 'applied' research and although both basic and applied research support conservation (Olupot and

Plumptre 2008), we summarise more of the research in which we could see results being used directly for park management. Researchers, protected area managers, and policy makers may be guided by lessons learnt and suggested lines of future investigation. The review also details site-specific details on history and biodiversity which may be of interest to a wide variety of audiences. The review mainly stems from scientific, peer-reviewed publications, but relevant information from reports, theses, field notes and documents written by the Uganda Wildlife Authority (UWA) is included.

Uganda's protected areas are a valid basis for such a review, as the country has a long history of ecological research. Some of the world's oldest permanent sample plots occur in the country's forests, dating back to 1933 (Eggeling, 1947; Sheil, 1996) and in this respect Uganda was well ahead of its time. Research in forests has improved forest management, leading to changes that influenced tropical forest management in other countries around the world (Dawkins and Philip, 1998).

Chapter 2

PARK SIZE, LOCATION AND HISTORY

This chapter summarizes information about each forest (figure 1) and details on the history of each site both before and after they were protected. This information is important for interpreting species composition and distribution patterns. Historical information also provides the hindsight needed for better management of these sites.

2.1. LOCATION

2.1.1. Bwindi Impenetrable National Park

Bwindi Impenetrable National Park (BINP) (0° 53'-1° 08'S, 29° 35'-29° 50'E) is on the highest block of the Kigezi highlands, at the edge of the Western Rift Valley. The park covers an area of 321 km^2. Parts of the western boundary lie along the border with the Democratic Republic of Congo (DRC).

2.1.2. Mgahinga Gorilla National Park

Mgahinga Gorilla National Park (MGNP) (1°23'S and 29°39'E) (33.7 km^2) is part of the once continuous forest cover that stretches from SW Uganda, the western parts of Rwanda and Burundi and eastern Democratic Republic of Congo (DRC). MGNP is in the extreme southwest of the country and abuts the much larger Parc National des Virunga in the DRC and Parc National des Volcans in Rwanda. MGNP and these two other parks form the trans-boundary conservation unit known as the Virunga Volcanoes (434km^2). The park is separated from Bwindi by 25 km of cultivation.

2.1.3. Kibale National Park

Kibale National Park (KNP) (795 km^2) in western Uganda, lies north east of Bwindi and 25 km east of the Rwenzori Mountains, just north of the equator (0°13' to 0°41'N and 30°19' to 30°32'E). It is contiguous with the northern end of Queen Elizabeth National Park, above the escarpment of the western Rift.

2.1.4. Rwenzori Mountains National Park

Rwenzori Mountains National Park (RMNP) (0°06':0°46'N, 29°47':30°11'E) is located along the Ugandan border with the DRC. The park covers much of the Rwenzori Massif above 1,600 m and totals an area of 998 km^2 in the districts of Kasese, Kabarole, and Bundibugyo. The mountain range runs over 100 km in a northeast-southwest direction and 50 km east to west. Eighty percent of the Massif is located in Uganda while the rest falls in the DRC. In the DRC, the mountains are part of the Parc National des Virunga.

2.1.5. Semliki National Park

Semliki National Park (SNP) lies along the Uganda-DRC border (0°44 to 0°53N and 29°57' to 30°11'E) (UWA 1996; UWA 2005), NW of the Rwenzori mountain range. It covers an area of 220 km^2 in Bundibugyo district and is continuous with the Ituri forest of the DRC across the Semliki river which forms the park's western boundary.

2.1.6. Mt Elgon National Park

Mt Elgon National Park (MENP) occurs on Mt Elgon which straddles the borders of Uganda and Kenya. It is the second highest mountain in Uganda (Margherita peak in the Rwenzori massif being the tallest) and the fifth highest in Africa with the peak rising to 4,320 m. The park is located in Kapchorwa and Mbale districts covering an area of 1,121 km^2 (UWA 2000a).

2.1.7. Budongo Forest Reserve

The Budongo Forest Reserve (BFR) is located close to the northern limit of the Western (Albertine) Rift between 1° 37'N-2° 03'N and 31° 22'-31° 46'E in a less densely populated part of the country (107 people/km^2 in 1991). The Reserve includes 790 km^2 of forest and grassland of which the forest covers 435 km^2 of a gently undulating terrain, with an overall downward slope from southeast to northwest, so that the 4 main rivers in the forest flow to the northwest (Reynolds 2005).

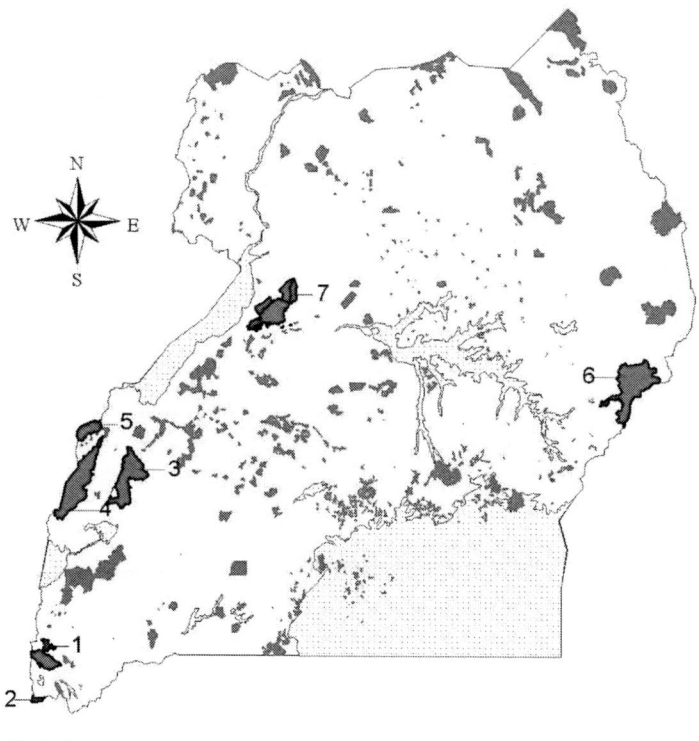

1- Bwindi Impenetrable National Park
2- Mgahinga Gorilla National Park
3- Kibale National Park
4- Rwenzori Mountains National Park
5- Semliki National Park
6- Mt. Elgon National Park
7- Budongo Forest Reserve

50 0 50 100 150 200 Kilometers

Figure 1. Map of Uganda's Forest reserves and Forest National Parks.

2.2. GENERAL HISTORY

No natural habitat is static, it is constantly changing, and there is a need to understand historical changes before we know how we want to manage it. Before formal management of forests by the Forest Department started in 1898, many forests had been set aside by ruling kings and chiefs as areas for sport hunting and important sources of meat, clothing, and medicine (Mwandha *et al.* 2003).

The forest department was however founded as part of a new Scientific and Forestry department which had been adopted by the British Government in 1894. During its first 30 years of existence, the department had no clear policy and concerned itself mainly with harvesting of forest produce, concentrating on wild rubber collection, pitsawing mahogany (*Khaya* and *Entandrophragma* spp.) in the Budongo forest, Mvule (*Milicia excelsa*) from the savanna and farmlands of Busoga, and the milling of *Podocarpus* spp. from the forests of south Masaka. The aims were, in part, to meet the needs of the First World War (Webster and Osmaston 2003). At the same time, the department also established plantations to provide fuel for brick-burning, tobacco-curing, and tea-drying, and for producing poles for telephone and electricity transmission. Origins of forest protected areas can be traced back to 1929 when the government first adopted a forest policy under which forest reserves were established and managed. However, no formal reservation and demarcation of forest reserves was made until 1932 during which time it was realized that it was necessary to declare and demarcate the existing natural forests as reserves and to prepare working plans.

The first forest policy of 1929 emphasized the use of forests for environmental protection. Forest reservation was achieved through negotiations with the Kingdom governments of Buganda, Toro, and Ankole, and district councils. These institutions agreed to cede the control of forest land to the protectorate government. Mabira and Mpigi forests and some forests adjacent to Lake Victoria were the first official forests, declared under the 1900 Buganda Agreement. By 1950, 7.9% of the land and swamp area of Uganda was demarcated as forest (Webster and Osmaston, 2003). Reserved forest included both major productive forests (such as Budongo) and large protective mountain forests that were reserved to protect watersheds (such as Rwenzori and Mt. Elgon). Working plans were prepared for the major forests, botanical and ecological surveys were made, and trials to improve regeneration were conducted. Additional existing unreserved forests were added to the forest estate over the next 15 years. By 1951, it was realized that the need for timber was much greater than the potential supply from the natural forests to meet the needs for Uganda's growing population and its rising living standards. This led to three approaches to forestry management: facilitation of forest regeneration after felling, planting of hardwoods, and setting up of exotic tree plantations. Attempts to increase stocking of high quality timber hardwoods had been made before (e.g. in Budongo they were started by 1922), through line planting and under-planting (Webster and Osmaston 2003). Revisions of the forest policy of 1929 in the 1950s emphasized short-term economic benefits from timber activities.

Although the main focus of forest management during its early years was sustainable exploitation, the future of Ugandan forests was bleakest during 1973-78 when the stated objective was to "capture" the returns to the nation from the utilization of the remaining forests (Howard 1991). Civil wars, lack of political will, and poor remuneration of staff during the regime of Idi Amin in the 1970s halted progress in management activities throughout Uganda's protected area system. In addition, there was widespread deforestation and land use change outside protected areas and encroachment by people into the forest reserves. By 1982, aerial counts and ecological assessment showed that Semliki Forest was extensively encroached and many trees had been felled; the southern sector of Kibale Forest was heavily settled with permanent buildings amongst areas of cultivation; and much of the forest on the lower slopes of Mt Elgon had disappeared (Eltringham and Malpas 1993).

After the fall of Idi-Amin's regime in 1979, significant conservation changes took place. In 1983, the Ugandan government initiated important steps in dealing with encroachment in forest reserves. The then minister of Agriculture and Forestry visited Kibale to see the problem there first hand. Efforts by this ministry were supported by that of Tourism and Wildlife which was responsible for the game reserve and corridor and shared administration of the Kibale Forest. People were successfully evacuated from Kibale and Mt Elgon, and the boundaries of the forest were redrawn in the case of Elgon.

Following the fall of the UPC government in 1986, evacuations from Kibale halted, and people reentered the reserve. Settlers were finally evicted from the reserve by the new government in 1992. Evacuations from other reserves were conducted at the same time, including the resettlement of people from an encroached 10 km^2 zone of Mgahinga Gorilla NP and relocation of communities settled near the headwaters of River Mbwa in Bwindi Impenetrable National Park. Since then, the environmental values have been restored in Kibale as well as other forests, first by a 1988 policy that re-emphasized these values, and subsequently re-emphasized by the National Forest Policy of 2002, and the National Forestry and Tree Planting Act of 2003 (Mwandha *et al.* 2003). Following evacuations at Kibale, the forest reserve was combined with the 206.5 km^2 of the game corridor to form Kibale National Park in 1993.

All of the present day forest parks in Uganda were converted from Central Forest Reserves to National Parks between May 1991 and September 1993. At that time, the National Parks moved away from pure protectionist policies and made significant moves toward participatory conservation, a trend that has continued within the Uganda Wildlife Authority created in 1996. Changes from forest reserves to national parks created numerous management challenges. As government forest reserves, the forests were managed to be selectively felled for timber and local communities were allowed to harvest firewood and other non-timber products. Although the Forest Department had established nature reserves (areas legally protected from all forms of exploitation) in central forest reserves, these areas were not very large and could not support species with large home ranges such as elephants, chimpanzees, and leopards. Because of their biological richness and conservation value, these forests were upgraded to the status of National Parks. With the re-designation as national parks, these forests effectively became completely protected with no access allowed. As such there was a lot of resentment amongst the local communities living next to these areas.

To minimize the friction between local people and the parks, complementary management mechanisms were developed, one of which was to initiate local participation and benefit sharing with communities for effective park management. Although the policy of benefit sharing started in Uganda in 1952, it was reviewed to give more benefit to residents neighboring reserves. In 1952 a portion of revenue from tourism and/or game license fees was given to districts, while the local residents neighboring reserves only benefited from the meat offered to them when the Game Department shot wildlife caught raiding farms (Archabald and Naughton-Treves, 2001). In the early 1990s this policy was expanded to harvesting of non-timber forest products. At Bwindi Impenetrable NP, where it was first initiated in Uganda, a pilot project for this process started in three parishes in 1992 with the help of CARE International, which had been developing a revenue sharing programme since 1988. At Mgahinga Gorilla NP, negotiations with the communities started in 1993. Harvesting of certain forest products under license began at Bwindi in late 1994. Since implementation of multiple use and collaborative management programs around Uganda's parks, relations between the parks and the communities have begun to improve.

2.3. SITE HISTORY

Forests vary as a result of differences in physical characteristics and disturbance history. It is important to have an understanding of disturbance and management history of the forests to better understand their ecology and how to manage them.

2.3.1. Bwindi Impenetrable National Park

BINP was formerly a forest reserve gazetted in 1932 for its ecological and economic importance and an animal sanctuary gazetted in 1961 (Leggat and Osmaston 1961). It consisted of two reserves then, known as Kasatoro and Kayonza crown forest reserves to the north and the south respectively. Demarcation of the boundaries was made between 1939 and 1947. Much of the boundary follows natural features such as rivers and roads and the international boundary with the DRC. Live markers, including exotic species such as *Cupressus* were planted where the boundary did not follow natural features. In 1942, the two forests were combined and gazetted as the Impenetrable Crown Forest. The primary aim of the animal sanctuary was to protect the population of gorillas. It was managed jointly by the Forest Department and Game Department until 1991 when it was made a national park (UWA 2000a).

The forest has a long history of human occupation dating to ca. 32,000-47,000 years ago (Cunningham, 1996), with Batwa peoples living in the forest. Forest clearance for agriculture outside Bwindi is thought to have begun about 2,200 years ago after the arrival of Bantu speaking peoples with iron-smelting technology. Two main ethnic groups living adjacent the forest are the Bakiga, traditionally agriculturalists, and the Batwa, previously forest dwellers, dependent mainly on hunting and gathering (Wild and Mutebi 1996).

Originally there were both Batwa and Bakiga households settled in many parts of the forest. Today, old settlement sites are often secondary forest planted with species of cultural significance (*Erythrina abyssinica* and *Ficus* sp.). In Mukono Parish along the northern edge of the southern sector, oral history has it that the first community members grouped together and moved to one site near the forest edge, to reduce leopard attack on livestock. Later the Forest Department negotiated a move from the gazetted forest to other land nearby that was forested. The Batwa remained in the forest longer, being more dependent on it than other groups. Some 100 Batwa lived nomadically in the forest in 1961, however it was illegal to do so as settlement and hunting was banned in the forest after it was gazetted as a reserve. The Forest Department moved the Batwa out in 1964. Using the forest as a base to rustle livestock made the Batwa increasingly unpopular with their neighbours (Wild and Mutebi 1996). The Batwa now live on land bought for them outside the forest by the Mgahinga Bwindi Impenetrable

Conservation Trust (MBIFCT). Cultivation was allowed in the forest until the 1980s under the taungya system involving interplanting food crops with timber trees.

When Bwindi became a Forest Reserve, it formed the central part of a large forest area which extended into the DRC. The forested land outside the Forest Reserve was held under customary tenure by individual families and was gradually cleared for timber and agriculture. The DRC part of the forest is more-or-less all gone apart from a small remnant in the Sarambwe Reserve. There is virtually no forest now remaining outside the park boundary (Wild and Mutebi 1996).

The Forest and Game Departments managed the forests under the Forest and Game Acts 1964. In Bwindi timber exploitation was officially limited to restricted species, felled by licensed pitsawyers. The Forest Act made provision for the local use of minor forest products (Butynski, 1984). Use of some products, particularly climbers, was controlled by issue of a free permit by the forest guards. The guards made their own assessments as to how many permits the resource could sustain and there was no control over the collection of medicinal plants (Wild and Mutebi 1996). In general, there was little control over resource harvesting, and more than 80% of the timber harvesting was illegal (Howard 1991). Between 512 and 1,049 people entered the forest daily to remove wood, bamboo, livestock forage, minerals, honey, and meat (Butynski 1984). By 1991, 61% of the forest was heavily logged, 29% selectively logged, and 10% remained essentially intact. As a result of uncontrolled exploitation, gap frequency and size in Bwindi is the largest known in tropical forests (Babaasa *et al.* 2001). In addition, two mammal species, the buffalo *Syncerus caffer* and leopard *Panthera pardus* (Butynski 1984) were hunted to extinction (Howard 1991).

When the forest was gazetted as a National Park in 1991, it incorporated 10 km^2 of the Mbwa River Tract which was not previously part of the Forest Reserve and was settled by people. All but one of the residents and cultivators reportedly had other lands and homes outside the tract (GEF 1995). It was believed that gorillas inhabiting this area would return if the natural vegetation was allowed to regenerate, and its accessibility makes it potentially very important as a gorilla tourism site. With assistance from GEF and the World Bank, Uganda National Parks agreed to provide cash compensation for structures, permanent crops, and for the current market value of the cultivated land. Compensation was given in 1996 and people moved out.

Today, lumbering is not legally permitted in the Park and illegal pitsawing is very rare. Other illegal activities, including encroachment occur at very low levels, and gold mining within the park boundaries is non-existent although freshly dug pits occasionally occur near the edge (Olupot 2004). Snares for antelopes are still set, especially in the southeastern part of the park (McNeilage *et al.* 1998; Olupot 2004) but are not as numerous as they were before the forest became a Park. Other threats to the park include fire outbreaks which were common in the past but are not as common now (Kasangaki *et al.* 2001), and the spread of exotic plants (Olupot 2004).

2.3.2. Mgahinga Gorilla National Park

MGNP was formerly an animal sanctuary gazetted in 1930, which became a game reserve in 1964. It was also gazetted as a forest reserve in 1941, and was jointly managed with the Game Department. In 1991, it was made a national park to protect mountain gorillas and the vulnerable populations of plants and animals endemic to the Albertine Rift (UWA 2000, 2001). Like BINP, MGNP has a long history of human occupation probably dating to *ca.* 32,000 – 47,000 years ago (Cunningham 1996). The main ethnic groups living around the park are the Bafumbira and Batwa. The Bafumbira are agriculturalists while the Batwa were previously forest dwellers dependent mainly on hunting and gathering (Wild and Mutebi 1996). The Batwa started moving out of both MGNP and BINP in the 1930s when the forests were gazetted as forest and game reserves and occupation and hunting were formally banned. They began spending more time as share-croppers and labourers on their neighbours' farms but still had access to many forest resources and the forests continued to be economically and culturally important to them before the areas were gazetted as parks (GEF 1995). Like Bwindi, the density of the human population around the park is among the highest on the African continent with up to 600 people per square kilometer..

While timber was the main forest product harvested from Bwindi, Bamboo (*Arundinaria alpina*) was the main resource harvested from Mgahinga. Bamboo harvests were thought to be very high between 1940 and 1950. The forest reserve was closed to Bamboo cutting from 1950-1955. In 1951, 10 km^2 of the forest reserve were degazetted due to a shortage of land caused by both immigrants from Rwanda and population growth. 220 families settled in the reserve growing mainly wheat and Irish potatoes. Encroachment on this conservation area was compounded by illegal activities including poaching of animals and bamboo harvesting. Bamboo cutting was closely regulated from 1955 with harvesting limited to two days per week and anyone caught illegally harvesting received rapid court action and heavy fines. Low salaries during the 1970s and early 80s removed the incentive for Game Department and Forest Department staff to function effectively and the low morale encouraged forest clearance and overexploitation (Wild and Mutebi 1996).

After a public inquiry preceding the establishment of the park, the boundary was re-established along the pre-1951 forest and game reserve boundary, and this was implemented in May 1991. The agreement with the local community leaders and the district administration included a planned relocation of reserve residents. The households were moved out and landowners stopped cultivating and grazing by the end of 1992. Compensation was made in May 1993. Moving communities out of the park increased the cost of hiring land outside the park by 1000%, the value of cattle fell as many were sold, milk prices increased, the supply of wheat straw used for thatching fell and the price increased (Wild and Mutebi 1996). In 1996, a multiple use zone was identified stretching 500 m from the park boundary, within which communities harvest bamboo rhizomes for planting outside the park, collect water, keep beehives, and harvest spear grass and medicinal plants (Wild and Mutebi 1996).

2.3.3. Kibale National Park

The area on which Kibale National Park is situated was previously settled. At the beginning of the 19th century, the area became infested with tsetse fly which brought sleeping sickness (Lang Brown and Harrop, 1962). The presence of fossil leaves on areas presently dominated by grassland indicates that the entire area once supported tropical high forest (Osmaston 1959, Wing and Buss 1970). Clearings that originated perhaps from volcanic activity were probably maintained through habitation and cultivation by people until they were driven out by sleeping sickness at the turn of the 20th century.

The Batoro, an ethnic group traditionally living around Kibale, are known not to usually destroy forest to cultivate, but prefer cultivating the elephant grass grassland on the hillsides. They also tend to avoid the forest edges to avoid baboons which raid fields. The usual practice of shifting cultivation was likely practiced in the area. As each plot became exhausted the family would open up fresh land, leaving the plot to be overrun by *Digitaria* and *Imperata* species which would slowly be replaced by elephant grass, *Pennisetum purpureaum*. Association of *Digitaria* and *Imperata* with shallow terraces confirm that cultivation was carried out in the grasslands within recent times (Lang Brown and Harrop, 1962). The local people traditionally used the forest as a sanctuary from attacks by other tribes before British rule. People dug pits with narrow circular mouths, widening out below the ground in which they stored grain and housed people in times of war (Lang Brown and Harrop 1962).

Kibale NP was gazetted as a forest reserve in 1932 and as a Central Forest Reserve in 1948. Timber was extracted commercially from the northern end of the forest from 1950 to the early 1970s. Before it was made a national park, Kibale was managed as a forest reserve in three distinct forest blocks delineated by roads. The north block, located to the north of the Kampala-Fort Portal road measured only 13.5 km^2. This block was selectively logged from 1950 to 1956. The northern part of the central block (361.5 km^2) was partly logged beginning in 1956 and continuing through to the late 1970s. The south block (184.5 km^2) which was demarcated from the central block by the Fort Portal- Kamwenge road, was not commercially logged (Wing and Buss 1970, Struhsaker 1997).

To facilitate tree regeneration and to protect experimental silvicultural plots in logged areas, elephants were excluded through regular patrols and scare-shooting (Wing and Buss, 1970). In the late 60s and early 70s, grasslands on hilltops in the northern part of the central block were planted with exotic trees (*Cupressus lusitanica, Pinus patula, Pinus carribea, Eucalyptus* sp., *Araucaria* sp.). Harvesting of these plantations started in 1992 and was complete by 2007. Beginning in 1971, people started settling in the park, and by 1982, 30,000 huts were present in 97 km^2 of the then Forest Reserve and the adjacent game corridor. In 1980, the human population within Kibale Forest and the game corridor exceeded 10,000 people and was perhaps as high as 17,000 (Van Orsdol 1986). These people were finally removed in 1992 in a process which proved to be controversial and created considerable animosity between local people and the Forest Department. Kibale was gazetted as a national park in 1993. The current size (766 km^2) is a result of merging the forest reserve (560 km^2) with the game corridor. Recent observations show formerly encroached areas rapidly regenerating to natural forest (Duncan and Chapman 2003 a,b, Omeja and Chapman unpublished data).

2.3.4. Rwenzori Mountains National Park

The area that is now Rwenzori National Park was initially North Ruwenzori and Ruwenzori Central Forest Reserves totaling an area of 970 km^2 (Leggat and Beaton 1961). The park is more-or-less linear but wider in the middle than at the extreme ends. At its establishment, the western boundary followed approximately the hill crests from the source of the Nyakibale to the source of the Mongiro rivers and was marked by cut lines and by trees, mostly *Eucalyptus globulus, Acacia dealbata, Cupressus lusitanica*, and *Erythrina abyssinica* planted singly at wide intervals along the line. The eastern boundary was a cut series of lines running at approximately the 2,100 m contour (*Ibid.*).

The park was established as a forest reserve in 1941 and was upgraded to a national park in 1991 to protect the mountains' role as Uganda's second largest water catchment after Mt Elgon. Agricultural lands surrounding the park are fed partly by the mountain run-off and partly from direct rainfall regulated by the forested slopes. The Rwenzoris with their glaciers at 5,100 metres (figure 2.) are the highest and most permanent sources of the River Nile and the source of the rivers Mobuku, Mongiro, Isolo, Rwimi, Lamya, Sebwe, Nyamwamba, and Nyamusagani (Leggat and Beaton 1961, Osmaston 1998). The Park's water catchment function benefits the fisheries of Lakes George and Edward, hydropower and irrigation schemes and provides water to over 500,000 surrounding people. River Mpanga, from which Fort Portal town draws its water, originates from the park and supplies this town and Kasese town also draws its water from rivers draining the park. Well known for mountaineering in Africa, it is an important area for tourism in Uganda (UWA 2000a, 2004).

Figure 2. The glaciers on the highest peaks of the Rwenzori Mountains National Park (D.Moyer/WCS).

This park has had little encroachment since its establishment. The main focus of management during earlier times was to improve tree cover over the area to forestall attempts to excise the reserve from the forest estate. Early burning from the top of the hills downwards rather than the reverse was recommended to be done annually. No exploitation was permitted in this reserve apart from traditional harvesting by Bakonjo and limited cutting by Kilembe mines (Leggat and Beaton 1961). Following the breakdown of law and order during the 1970s and 1980s, the integrity of the montane forest zone was violated by intensive hunting of mammals for bushmeat (elephant, buffalo, duiker, hyraxes, and monkeys). The damage caused by the extraction of other resources has been less severe. Denudation, burning and erosion of the foothills outside the park boundary stand as a reminder of what could occur as the human population density around the forest grows (the current density now ranges between 150 and 430 persons/km^2) (IUCN 1994b).

Hunting pressure in this park is very high and poachers have removed most of the large mammals (e.g. Olupot et al. 2008) from the main valleys while cultivation of the ever steeper land below the protected area boundary caused serious soil erosion. In 1997, the park was closed to tourists due to insurgency but was reopened in July 2001 after the Allied Democratic Forces, a rebel group opposing the government, were pushed into the DR Congo (UWA 2004).

2.3.5. Semliki National Park

The area that constitutes the park was gazetted as a forest reserve in 1932, in part to control the spread of sleeping sickness and yellow fever and was made a National Park in 1993. Introduction of the taungya system of management by the forest department led to serious encroachment, and between 1975 and 1983, 25,000 people in 1,500 families lived in the reserve. All illegal settlers were evicted in the early 1990s before the area was declared a national park. By 2003, some 20-40 Batwa families still lived within the park (Lamprey et al. 2003). 85 people (Batwa) still live in this park today (Aggrey Rwetsiba, pers.comm). The population density of people on the public land adjoining the park is high (>300 per km^2) and increasing at a rate of 3.4% per year. The park is exploited by local communities for bushmeat, poles, fuelwood, and medicinal plants. Hunting pressure is high. The park is regionally important for biodiversity conservation. Commercially, the park has a high potential for bird tourism because it has many species from the Congo basin forests which in East Africa can only be viewed here.

2.3.6. Mt Elgon National Park

The park was originally a central forest reserve gazetted in 1938. It was declared a national park in 1993 (UWA 2000a) and was approved as a UNESCO Man and Biosphere Reserve in 2005. Areas surrounding the park are densely populated, and the population density on the slopes in Mbale district reached 512 people km^{-2} in 2000 (UBOS 2001). Communities adjacent to the park make extensive use of the forest edge areas for firewood, poles, medicines, and bamboo as a source of food. Hunting was traditionally important as a source of income although large mammal populations are now drastically reduced. More than one million people depend on the conservation of this park as a water source.

Parts of the park are encroached. Encroachment in the park started in the late 1960s when persistent raiding by the Karimojong forced the Sabiny people up the mountain. The population of immigrant people increased in the reserve over the following years alongside an increase in the numbers of the Benet pastoralists who traditionally grazed their cattle in the clearings in the northern areas; forcing park authorities to excise an area of about 75 km^2 from the park (UWA 2000b).

2.3.7. Budongo Forest Reserve

Budongo forest (793 km^2) is the largest forest reserve in Uganda under the management of the National Forestry Authority (NFA) (Forest Department, 2002). The forest consists of a main block of 364 km^2 (Budongo) and smaller blocks 66 km^2 (Siba), 95 km^2 (Kitigo), and 268 km^2 (Kaniyo-Pabidi) (Howard 1991). It is important for timber production, being rich in timber species with high quality mahogany trees. It is also important for biodiversity conservation, ranking third in Uganda in this respect (Forest Department 2002). Unlike Kibale, Bwindi, and other forests in Uganda, Budongo was not settled at the time it was gazetted as a forest reserve and has not been encroached. Trypanosomiasis, which entered Bunyoro from north of the Nile in 1904 and decimated human and cattle populations, has been linked to the colonial administrators effort to stop the practice of grassland burning which was a tradition among local herders. In response to this disease, the administration evacuated people from large parts of Bunyoro in 1909-1912 and shot most of the wild animals for the fear that they harbored the trypanosomes. Only elephants were spared because they provided revenue from Sport Hunting.

The area that is presently Budongo Forest Reserve underwent increases and decreases in tree cover during pre-historic times. Dry conditions of the last ice age that occurred 18,000 years ago reduced forest cover to a level much smaller than it is today. Medium altitude forest increased during the early Holocene from around 11,000 years ago and there was evidence of forest disturbance by humans in the late Holocene, 2,300 years ago. Forest cover appears to have reached a maximum 7,000-5,000 years ago, but the dry period from 1,000-700 years ago likely reduced the forest cover again. Thus, along the Albertine rift axis from the southwest to the north east, forests waxed and waned in size. With wetter conditions, species re-entered from eastern DR Congo through the southwestern forests, and the forests again expanded (Reynolds 2005). Compared to forests in the southwestern part of the country, Budongo is rich in tree species, having the highest (449) number of any forest in Uganda (Plumptre *et al.* 2003b).

The reserve was established in parts, from 1932 to 1968 and is marked with earth corner cairns, concrete corner beacons and directional trenches (Forest Department 2002). The northeastern part of the forest reserve is dually managed by NFA and UWA. The forest has historically been managed for timber production. Limited pitsawing and rubber tapping started in 1907 and planting of mahoganies in 1924 and sawmilling started in 1926. From the start, Budongo Forest was managed with the aim of producing a sustainable supply of timber over the long term. Scientific management started with the idea that mahoganies and other valuable timber trees in Budongo might be subject to eventual competitive exclusion by the slower growing *Cynometra alexandri* that could survive in lower light conditions (Eggeling 1947; Harris 1934). Initially mahogany seedlings were planted in harvested areas and game scouts shot animals, particularly elephants, that ventured near the planted areas to consume the saplings that emerged. However, research showed that most seedlings that were planted died, because of poor light or smothering by climbers, and it was decided to encourage natural regeneration instead.

It turned out that leaving the forest to produce its own crop of young trees and then opening the canopy around them, weeding, and removing understorey climbers and other impediments to the growth of young mahoganies was a better method to regenerate the mahoganies. Poisoning of non-commercial trees (especially the strangler figs, *Celtis*, *Cynometra*, and *Lasiodiscus* species) with arboricide (2-4,5T or 'Agent Orange') was used to open up the canopy to give the mahoganies more light. The results of these efforts are known to have been dramatic. The *Cynometra* forest which was dominant in 1951 is much reduced and mixed forest predominates today (Plumptre, 1996).

At this time there was also a move towards longer felling cycles from about 40 years towards a monocyclic 70 years which would have the logging operation going back to the same concession every 70 years. This results in heavier felling (equivalent to arboricide treatment) in each cycle to open up the canopy, but still involved keeping seed trees and only felling harvested species over a prescribed breast height diameter.

Research during the '60s at Nakawa (Forest Department's Sawmill and Research unit in Kampala) showed that more could be made out of timber harvested in the forest resulting in less waste:

- It was possible to saw and market many more natural forest species so it was no longer necessary to kill trees with arboricide. They could be sawn and increase timber yield per hectare without any further adverse effect on the forest.
- During preservation trials with vacuum-pressure methods it was found that almost all non durable timbers were permeable to preservation treatments so timber for any use could be made to last longer.
- Trials with the Nakawa sawmill were carried out in sawing different species and finding suitable uses for them. This included eucalyptus and the softwoods grown in plantations
- Trials were carried out on sawing smaller logs including branchwood of larger trees to increase the efficiency of utilisation of the resource.
- A wheeled logging skidder was obtained and caused much less damage to the forest floor than tracked tractors.
- Research on charcoal burning with small circular metal kilns showed it was possible to use branchwood from trees felled for timber to make charcoal more efficiently than earth kilns and a wood wool machine showed that it was possible to make wood wool from "waste" branchwood which could make wood wool-cement slab which could then be used to make the walls of timber framed houses or roof insulation for tin-roofed houses.

Although mahoganies (*Khaya* and *Entandrophragma*) have been the main target of felling programs in Budongo, other valuable woods like *Milicia* and *Maesopsis* have also been removed for furniture and house construction, *Cynometra* for flooring and bridge construction, and *Cordia millenii* for dug-out canoes. Today, the removal of mahoganies continues both illegally and as a planned management activity. Although these activities continue to cream-off the most valuable timber trees, the biggest single cause of change to the composition and dynamics of the forest in the'50s and early '60s was the use of arboricides to remove non-utilisable "weed trees" and encourage regeneration of marketable species.

Chapter 3

PARK ENVIRONMENT- PHYSICAL AND BIOLOGICAL CHARACTERISTICS

Uganda's forests are very variable in structure and composition. In geological history, as global climate has changed, these forests experienced periods when they were joined to the main forest of the Congo Basin and periods when they have been isolated and fragmented. They are located on different landforms, at different altitudes with differing geological histories, soil characteristics, and weather patterns. Because of the variation of these physical characteristics, intrinsic differences in biological composition can be expected as biological organisms respond to the physical environment they live in, leading to a great variation in species diversity in this part of Africa.

3.1. BWINDI IMPENETRABLE NATIONAL PARK

3.1.1. Physical Environment

The Bwindi landscape is very rugged, with numerous steep-sided hills and narrow valleys formed from up-warping of the Western Rift Valley. The only relatively flat area within the park is Mubwindi swamp (1 km^2) in the southern sector. The park is an important catchment area for the surrounding agricultural communities. The main flow of waters out of the park drain into the rivers Ndeego, Ruheza-Myenda (Shongi) with a tributary originating from L. Bunyonyi, Kashasha, Ivi in the south; and Ishasha, Mbwa, Munyaga and Ntengyere in the north. Ruheza-Myenda and Ndeego flow into Lake Mutanda while the rest drain into Lake Edward to the north. The forest tilts gently northwest and northward with the highest point (2,607 m) being in the southeastern corner and the lowest (1,190 m) at a point where the River Ishasha emerges out of the park.

The soils are mainly tropical red earths with an overlying layer of brown to black spongy humus. They are deep and rich. Acidity ranges from pH 2.9 to pH 5.2. They are moderately poor in structure, loose and friable when dry and highly susceptible to erosion when vegetation cover is removed. In swampy valley bottoms, blue to grey clays occur often overlaid with a layer of peat. Underlying rocks consist of Precambrian shale, phyllite, quartz, quartzite, schist and granite of the Karagwe-Ankolean system (Leggat and Osmaston 1961).

The park is broadly classified as a medium to high altitude forest. March-April and September-November are the wettest months, while December-January and June-August are the driest. The annual mean temperature range is 7-15°C minimum to 20-27°C maximum, and annual precipitation ranges from 1,130-2,390 mm (Howard 1991). Coldest periods occur during the dry season months of June and July. Set in an area with a large rural population (200-400 people km^{-2}, compared with the national average of 88 people km^{-2}), the park boundary is typically an abrupt transition from forest to a matrix of cultivated lands and settlements (figure 3). With establishment of National Park status, protection of the forest is now total, with limited extraction of weaving materials and medicinal plants and beekeeping by local communities under agreements with the park.

3.1.2. Biological Environment

Bwindi is one of the few large forests in East Africa where mid altitude and montane vegetation communities overlap. At 1500 m, the forest is dominated by *Parinari excelsa*, grading into *Newtonia buchananii* at 2000 m and *Chrysophyllum gorungosanum* at 2,200 m (Howard 1991). *Arundinaria alpina* (bamboo) is restricted to a tiny 1 km^2 area to the southeast, at elevations higher than 2400 m.

Because of its wide elevation range, and its probable role as a Pleistocene refugium during the last ice age, the forest has extremely high biodiversity with many endemic species of plants and animals for the Albertine Rift. Bwindi has the highest diversity of mammal species among Uganda's parks, with a total of 135 species recorded with 10 primates. It also has the highest total plant species richness with 1,405 species recorded (Plumptre et al. 2007). Bwindi is second to Budongo for the number of tree species (at least 393 recorded, table 1) and ferns (more than 104 species). 10 tree species in this forest occur nowhere else in Uganda and 17 others have a limited distribution in the country.

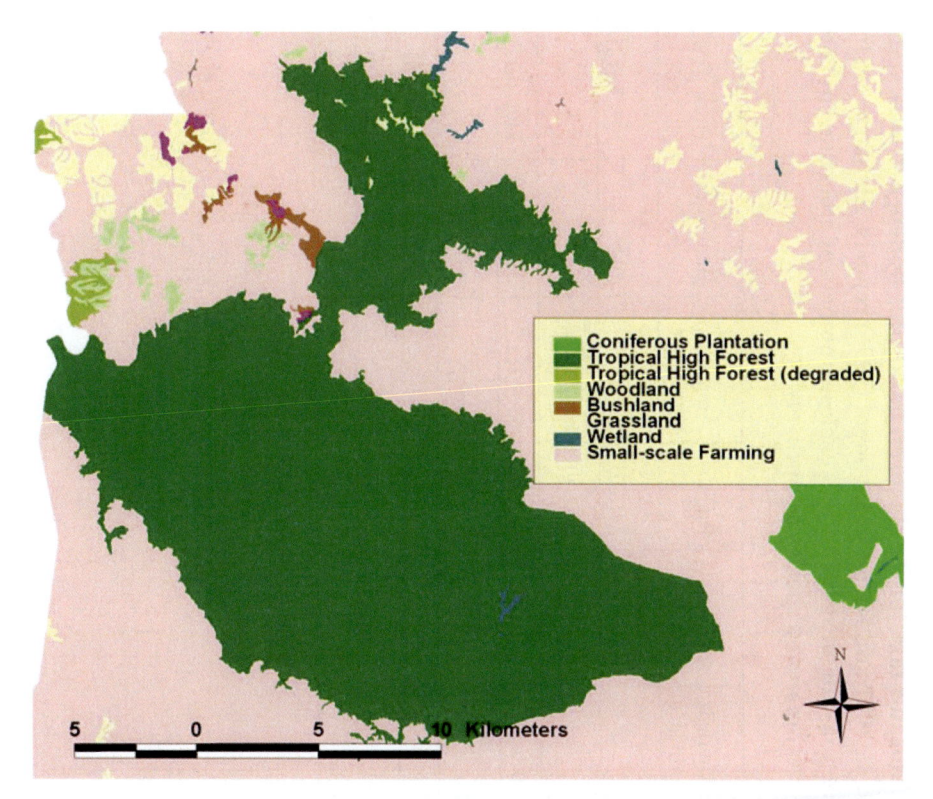

Figure 3. Map of Bwindi Impenetrable National Park and the surrounding area showing the major vegetation types. Bwindi has a very hard boundary with cultivation.

One species, *Lovoa swynnertonnii* is globally threatened (IUCN 1994a). Bwindi is also the richest forest in Uganda in terms of bird species, supporting 381 (Plumptre et al. 2003b).

Table 1. Species numbers for the main indicator taxa for the six forest parks plus Budongo. Unless stated otherwise, numbers were taken from Plumptre _et al_. 2007 and Forest department (1996) reports. Blank spaces indicate taxa and locations for which numbers were unavailable. Parentheses enclose numbers of albertine rift endemics and threatened species respectively

Site	All mammals	Diurnal primates	Birds	Reptiles	Amphibians	Butterflies	Trees	All plants[1]
Bwindi Impenetrable National Park	135(20,7)	7	381(24,6)	34(6,0)	29(6,6)	202	393(74,18)	1405
Mgahinga Gorilla National Park	76	3	185 (14,4)					
Kibale National Park	115(5,7)	9	327(3,3)	56(3,0)	33(5,3)	221	330(16,12)	532
Rwenzori Mountains National Park	102(18,10)	4	241(21,4)	34(9,0)	25(7,1)	78	199(55,5)	696
Semliki National Park	86(1,5)	8	441(7,9)	49(0,0)	24(1,0)	309	318(7,14)	333
Mt Elgon National Park		3				182		
Budongo Forest Reserve	95(0,5)	5	362(0,1)	48(1,0)	32(1,1)	289	449(29,18)	1064

[1]Plant species include trees, shrubs, herbs, ferns, and climbers.

The forest has 202 species of butterfly (84% of the country's total) (Plumptre *et al.* 2003b) and may be the most important forest in Africa for the conservation of montane butterflies. Thirty three species of amphibians, and 34 reptile species also occur in Bwindi (Plumptre *et al.* 2003b). About half (325-340) of the world's population of mountain gorillas (Alastair McNeilage pers. comm.) and a reasonable population (213) of chimpanzees (Plumptre *et al.* 2003a) occur here. Cape buffalo and the leopard are known to be extinct from this park, and the giant forest hog has not been sighted in the park for many years, but 20-30 elephants (Babaasa 2000) still inhabit the park and the park is important for conservation of the black-fronted duiker *Cephalophus nigrifrons* (Lamprey *et al.* 2003). Of particular concern are species such as the African Green Broadbill (*Pseudocalyptomena graueri*) which is recorded from here and only two other sites in the world and Grauer's Rush Warbler (*Bradypterus graueri*) which is restricted to montane swamps along the border of Uganda and Rwanda with DRC. The forest has 19 threatened vertebrates and 18 threatened plants (Plumptre et al. 2003).

3.2. MGAHINGA GORILLA NATIONAL PARK

3.2.1. Physical Environment

The park has three extinct volcanoes and the elevation of the park rises from 1,117 m in the north to 4,127 m at the summit of Mt Muhabura. The terrain consists mostly of gentle slopes rising gradually from the northern edge and then steeply from the bottom of the three volcanoes that are lined up along the border of Uganda. Mt Muhabura is easternmost, and the youngest, while the oldest of the three mountains is Mt Sabinyo (3,645 m) which lies to the west. Mt. Gahinga (3,475 m) is located between the two. Numerous caves occurring on the mountain slopes were derived from lava tubes created during the volcanic activity of the early to mid-Pleistocene.

MGNP experiences two wet and two dry seasons. The wettest months are March-April, and September-December, while the driest are January-February and May-August. It is frequently shrouded in mist and humidity is high. Average rainfall is about 1650 mm per year (Werikhe 1991), but there is considerable inter-year variability. Temperatures range from 4°C at the highest elevations to 18°C at the lowest. The deep porous volcanic soils do not retain water through the dry season, making the risk of fire outbreaks during the dry season particularly high.

With three main rivers and two high altitude swamps, the park is an important catchment for the communities. River Nyakigezi originates from Mt Sabinyo and flows out of the park near the Uganda-DRC border into the DRC. River Ntebeko originates from the swamp in the saddle between Gahinga and Sabinyo, flows through the park headquarters and south into Lake Mutanda. River Kabiranyuma originates from the Kabiranyuma swamp in the saddle between Mt. Muhabura and Gahinga. Although the source of the large underground river Chuho, from which Kisoro town obtains its water, is unknown, it is likely that it is at least partly supplied by waters from MGNP.

3.2.2. Biological Environment

MGNP, like BINP, is thought to have been part a refugium extending from eastern DRC to parts of western Uganda during the late Pleistocene. Its species diversity is believed to be high, but recording is incomplete. The vegetation of much of MGNP is degraded. The 10 km^2 area encroached during the 1950s has not fully recovered its vegetation and is currently a mosaic of grassland, bamboo, *Hypericum*, and exotic trees (figure 4). A small area of pure montane forest occurs at the base of Mt Muhabura while the rest of the park contains alpine and sub-alpine vegetation types. The vegetation of the intact forest comprises *Hagenia-Hypericum* montane forest and *Arundinaria alpina* bamboo at lower altitudes to giant *Lobelia* and giant *Senecio* forest with open moorland and high altitude swamp vegetation (Kingdon 1967, Byaruhanga *et al.* 2001). The bamboo zone stretches from Mt Sabinyo to the lower slopes of Mt. Muhabura. On Mt Sabinyo, the montane forest zone occurs above the bamboo zone while on Mt Gahinga, it occurs below it (UWA 2001).

Mgahinga is considered to be regionally important for biodiversity conservation. It has 76 mammal species notably the buffalo, elephant, black-fronted duiker, bushbuck, giant forest hog, leopard, and the spotted hyena. The park only has two primate species; mountain gorillas and golden monkeys (*Cercopithecus mitis kandti*). Both are of conservation concern with the golden monkey effectively restricted to the Virunga Volcanoes region and the mountain gorilla restricted to the Virunga Volcanoes and Bwindi. One hundred and eighty five bird species have been recorded in the park (Kalina 1991). Mgahinga's protective vegetation cover makes the park an important catchment area for water for Kisoro district (UWA 2000a, 2001).

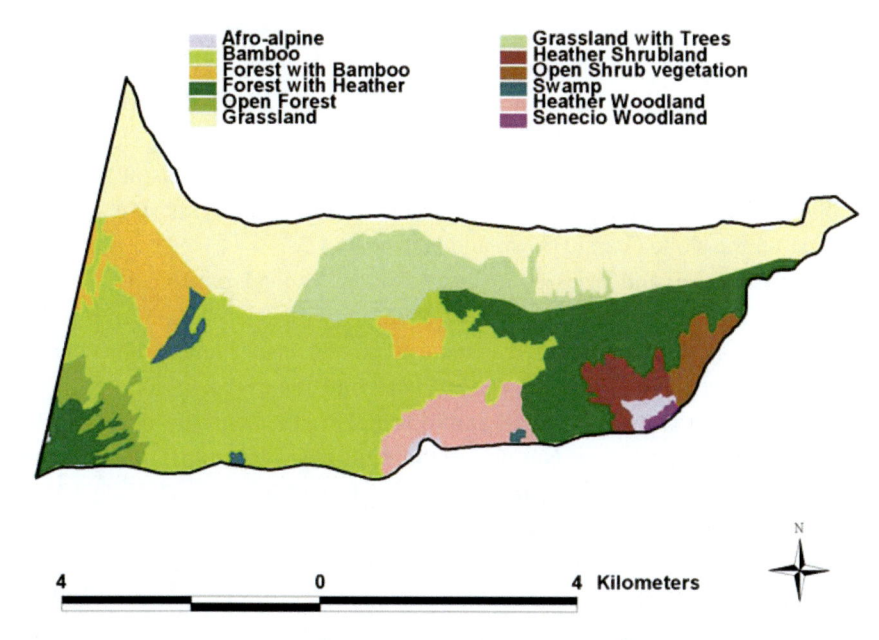

Figure 4. Map of the main vegetation types in Mgahinga Gorilla National Park. Where the park was cultivated in the north, it has reverted to grassland and grassland with trees.

3.3. KIBALE NATIONAL PARK

3.3.1. Physical Environment

The physical environment of Kibale comprises rolling hills, ranging from 1,110 m in the south, to 1,590 m in the north and is drained by two main rivers, Mpanga and Dura which flow into Lake George. Much of the area that currently comprises the park was probably destroyed by volcanic activity in the past. The area is underlain by Precambrian rocks of the Toro system. The rocks consist of undifferentiated acid gneisses of the basement complex, while prominent ridges are mostly composed of crystalline quartzites that vary widely in structure. Purplish low-grade schists and phyllites occur on some hills. Granites, gneisses and amphibolites are intruded into the quartzites (Lang Brown and Harrop, 1962). Rock outcrops occur but are not common (Wing and Buss 1970).

The soil is well drained, predominantly red and ferralitic, consisting of sandy loams and sandy clay loams (Wing and Buss 1970). The soil catena consists of three distinct series. Soils on flat crests of higher hills are derived from laterite, while the thin, gritty, stony soil on the steep upper slopes of the laterite capped hills is derived from quartzite. Below the quartzite soils, the soil is deep red and clayey, extending to the valley bottom where it is overlain by a thin layer of black clayey soil (Lang Brown and Harrop, 1962). Valley bottom soils are generally acid and poor in exchangeable bases, while those in the grasslands at the hilltop have high levels of phosphorus. The level of soil fertility is fair to good, increasing up the slope (Lang Brown and Harrop 1962).

Kibale is cooler and drier compared to other tropical rainforests (Richards 1964 cited in Struhsaker 1997). Rainfall occurs in two peaks, with March to May and September-November being the wettest months, and January and July the driest. El Nino years are unusually wetter. Data collected over a period of 20 years (1977-1989) show that mean annual rainfall is higher at Kanyawara in the north of the forest (1,622 mm) than Ngogo in the centre (1,492 mm). Mean annual precipitation has been increasing over the years, from 1,378 mm in 1903-1912 to 1,666 mm in 1983-1991 (Struhsaker 1997).

Between 1990 and 2005 the area near Kanyawara received an average of 1702 mm of rainfall annually. Today this region receives approximately 300 mm more rainfall/annum than it did a century ago. Other climatic changes include: less frequent droughts, an earlier onset of the rainy season, and a 4.4 C^o increase in average maximum monthly temperature. This temperature change has occurred over the last 40 years and is much higher than current global averages for other areas (Chapman and Chapman unpublished data).

The trend, though not similar to the records from sub-saharan west Africa, tallies with models of global circulation which predict changes in the intensity of equatorial rainfall in response to global warming. According to the models, increases in atmospheric carbon dioxide levels will increase rainfall intensity near the equator and decrease it in areas peripheral to the equator (Struhsaker 1997), although not uniformly so throughout—east and central Africa are for instance expected to receive more than normal rainfall, large portions of the Sahel less, while the situation in west Africa will be complex with some areas receiving more, and others less rain than normal (Hulme et. al. 2001 and IPCC 2001 reviewed by Sinibaldi et al. 2004). In Kibale, mean annual temperatures are slightly higher at Ngogo than Kanyawara (24.2^o vs. 23.3^o). Inter-monthly variations in both rainfall and temperature are also greater during El Nino years (Struhsaker 1997).

3.3.2. Biological Environment

The Park is classified as a medium altitude tropical moist forest and 351 tree species have been recorded. Forest (57.9%) and grassland (14.6%) excluding what used to be the Game corridor are the most extensive habitats in Kibale. Grasslands were much more common in the southern sections of the national park than in the northern areas. Woodlands are prevalent in the far south of the park, but they only cover 5.8% of the total park's surface area (figure 5). Wetlands and lakes comprise 2.2% of the park and are distributed throughout the area [Osmaston, 1959; Kingston, 1967]. Plantations constituted 1.0% of the park's area [Struhsaker *et al.*, 1989; Chapman and Chapman, 1996; Struhsaker, 1997; Zanne, 1998].

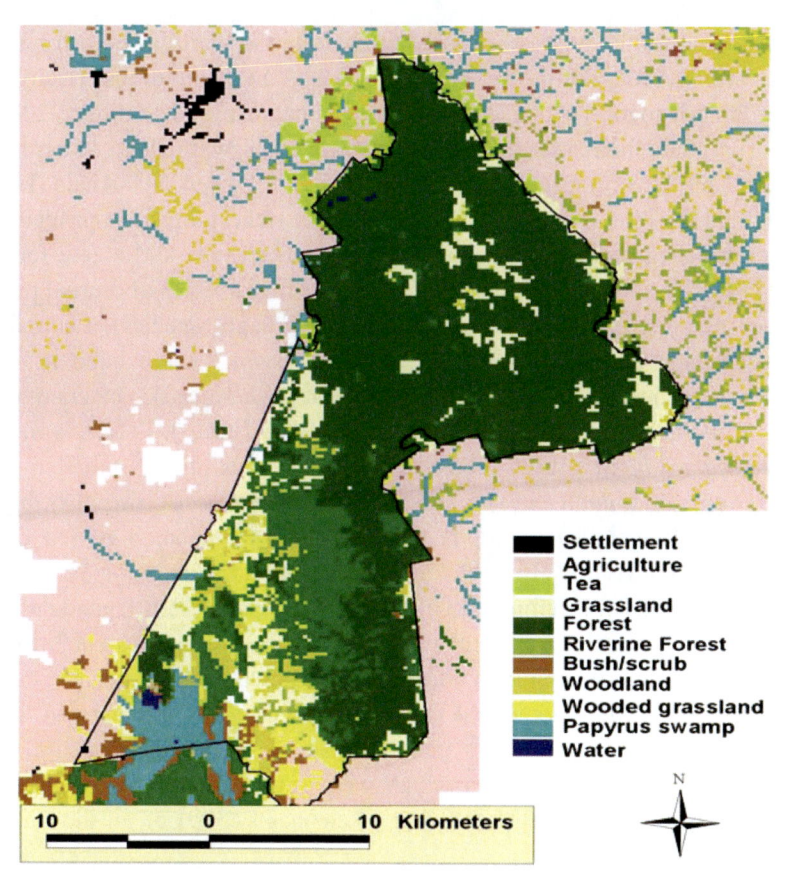

Figure 5. Map of the main vegetation types in Kibale National park. Note the woodland and grassland in the centre of the park and in the area(corridor) to the south west that links Kibale with Queen Elizabeth National Park.

They have been harvested, and there has been substantial regeneration of disturbed forest and savannas to natural forest (e.g. Laporte 2008). Abandoned farms (10.3%) and degraded forest (8.7%; largely representing secondary forest associated with agricultural encroachment) cover 146 km^2. Seventy-six percent of these degraded lands were found in the southern corridor (Chapman and Lambert 2000). Park vegetation is diverse, and is dominated by *Parinari* in the north, *Piptadeniastrum* and *Pterygota* in the central area, and *Cynometra* in the south.

Kibale National Park supports a rich fauna with 327 bird species (Plumptre et al. 2007) of at least 46 families (Van Orsdol, 1986). Kibale has the highest recorded number of reptile and amphibian species of any Ugandan Park (Plumptre et al. 2007) and the highest number of diurnal primate species recorded for any site in the country.

The forest has the highest recorded biomass in the world of both frugivorous (Kanyawara: 1,116kg/km^2' Ngogo: 754kg/km^2) and folivorous (Kanyawara: 1,214kg/km^2; Ngogo: 1200kg/km^2) primates (Chapman and Lambert, 2000). In terms of primate biomass, it is only rivalled by Tiwai Island, Sierra-Leone (folivores: 600kg/km^2; frugivores: 786kg/km^2); followed by Kuala Lompat, Malaysia (933kg/km^2 overall). Kibale is one of the richest forests in primate fauna in Africa, rivalled only by Semliki NP in western Uganda and a few forests in eastern DRC, Rwanda and West Africa. There are nine species of diurnal primates and three nocturnal (potto and two bushbaby (Galago) species). Diurnal ones include: Chimpanzees (*Pan troglodytes schweinfurthii*), olive baboons (*Papio anubis*), grey-cheeked mangabeys (*Lophocebus albigena*), black-and-white colobus (*Colobus guereza*), red colobus (*Procolobus badius*), l'Hoest's monkeys (*Cercopithecus l'hoesti*), blue monkeys (*Cercopithecus mitis*), redtail monkeys (*Cercopithecus ascanius*), and vervet monkeys (*Cercopithecus aethiops*). Its large population of *Procolobus badius* is the only viable population of red colobus remaining in Uganda. It is also well known for its research on chimpanzees and is the most popular site for chimpanzee viewing in Uganda with Uganda's largest population, estimated at 1,429 chimpanzees (Plumptre *et al.* 2003a). Other mammals include buffalo, hippo, bushbuck, and two duiker species; the blue duiker *Cephalophus monticola* and the red duiker *Cepholophus natalensis*. Rare mammals include giant forest hogs, pangolins, sitatungas, and golden cats. It is an important sanctuary for elephants which were severely reduced in Uganda by poaching. Kibale has the largest number of elephants (390) of all the forests in Uganda (Wanyama 2005).

3.4. RWENZORI NATIONAL PARK

3.4.1. Physical Environment

The main distinction of the Rwenzori is the scenically spectacular nature of its high peaks and the presence of snow fields and glaciers. Mount Kilimanjaro and Mount Kenya have similarities with the Rwenzoris. Rwenzori is a range of mountains with an alpine area of greater extent and higher species diversity (IUCN 1994). The range is steep and rugged, rising from about 1,600m to 5,109m asl. At the centre are 6 high peaks: Mt Stanley (5,109m), Mt Speke (4,890m), Mt Baker (4,843m), Mt. Emin (4,798m), Mt Gessi (4,715m), and Mt Luigi di Savoia (4,627m) (Leggat and Beaton 1971). Margherita peak (5,109) on Mt Stanley makes the Rwenzoris the third highest mountain in Africa after Mt Kilimanjaro (5,895m) and Mt Kenya (5,200m). Peat bogs up to 6 feet deep are common at altitudes over 3,000m (UWA 2004).

The mountain is derived from an old basement system of Precambrian rocks uplifted by the tectonic movements responsible for the formation of the western rift valley. The range is mostly composed of granites, gneisses and quartzites of the basement complex, while at the centre of the range is the Rwenzori Group, a band of schists and resistant volcanics of which the latter form the steep peaks of Mt. Stanley at the centre of the range and the Portal peaks outside the main range.

Glaciation in the last 300,000 years has left moraines which form important landscape features such as the Nyabitaba ridge and Lake Mahoma. Glaciers though are receding with global warming and are expected to disappear by 2023 (Mileham et al. in prep). Recent (5,000-10,000 years ago) volcanic eruptions left explosion craters east and south of the range (Osmaston 2006). Soils are derived from Precambrian rocks and are generally of low fertility. They show a marked altitudinal zonation. Lower grass slopes usually have moderately acidic soils yellow or brown in color. On gentler upper slopes, the soils are more acidic, leached, with low fertility owing to greater rainfall. Higher up, soil is mostly sandy or stony with good drainage. The park has two rainy seasons, from March to May and from August to December and most of the plains at the foot lie in a rain shadow, getting as little as 750mm of rain a year. Minimum and maximum temperatures at Bujuku huts are -1^0C and 7^0C and the seasonal variation is slight (Osmaston 2006).

3.4.2. Biological Environment

RNP is very important for biodiversity conservation, being part of the Albertine rift. It contains exceptional biological value as it has particularly distinct flora and, to a lesser extent, fauna. Due to higher precipitation (2,500 mm year^{-1}), the Rwenzori mountains have the most extensive area of tropical montane cloud forest in the region. Mount Kenya and the other eastern African mountains are all exceeded in biological and geological variety by the Rwenzori, being a centre of endemism for the region (IUCN 1994b). The flora are unusual, and include many species endemic to the Albertine Rift in the higher altitude zones. Most significant are the giant heathers, groundsels, ericas and lobelias of the tree heath and alpine zones. Vegetation depends largely on altitude. The park has several distinct vegetation zones which replace each other with altitude (figure 6).

The broken montane forest dominated by *Symphonia globulifera, Prunus, Arundinaria alpina, Albizia* and *Dombeya* spp occurs at about 2,400 m (Forest Department, 1996b). 199 tree species (18% of the country's total) have so far been recorded in this zone. Next is the a bamboo (*Arundinaria alpina*) forest up to an altitude of 3,000 m, a heather zone dominated by giant heathers such as *Phillipia trimera* and small trees such as *Hagenia* and *Rapanea*, frequently over 10 m in height up to 3,800 m, and afro-alpine moorland that ends at the snowline at 4,400 m (Leggat and Beaton 1961).

The park contains 241 species of birds (27% of the country's total), and 78 species of butterfly. Although none of these species are unique to the Rwenzori, many are endemic to the Albertine Rift region. A study of invertebrate life forms in the alpine zone listed 60 species, 25 of which were new to science, indicative of a much more extensive fauna waiting to be discovered (IUCN 1994b).

One hundred and two mammal species have been recorded in the park. The Rwenzori duiker *Cephalophus rubidus* is found nowhere else in the World and the Rwenzori otter shrew *Micropotamogale ruwenzorii* is only known from here and Nyungwe National Park in Rwanda. The park has elephant, giant forest hog, and sitatunga in small numbers and buffaloes, which had once disappeared, have re-appeared. Hyrax and leopards also occur in the park as well as four species of diurnal primate: the common chimpanzee (currently estimated at 500 individuals, Plumptre *et al.* 2003a) found in the lower altitude forest areas, a subspecies of the Angola colobus (*Colobus angolensis ruwenzorii*), the Rwenzori colobus, restricted to this park, l'Hoests monkey and the blue monkey. Biodiversity is extraordinarily high, with 17 regionally endemic birds and 12 regionally endemic mammals. The elephant, common chimpanzee and l'hoests monkey are globally threatened (IUCN 1994b). Because of its physical and biological values, RNP was recognized as a World Heritage Site in 1994. Among rare reptiles, the strange-nosed chameleon *Bradypodion xenorhinum* is endemic to the Rwenzoris.

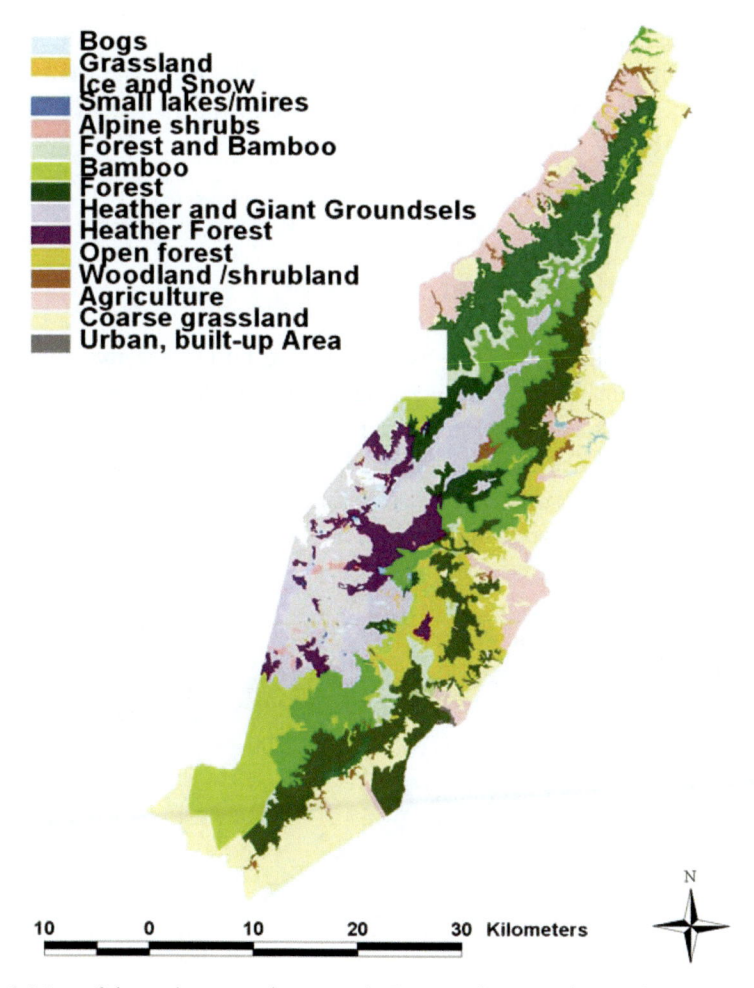

Bogs
Grassland
Ice and Snow
Small lakes/mires
Alpine shrubs
Forest and Bamboo
Bamboo
Forest
Heather and Giant Groundsels
Heather Forest
Open forest
Woodland /shrubland
Agriculture
Coarse grassland
Urban, built-up Area

10   0   10   20   30 Kilometers

N

Figure 6. Map of the main vegetation types in Rwenzori Mountains National Park.

3.5. SEMLIKI NATIONAL PARK

3.5.1. Physical Environment

The park lies on flat to gently undulating land on the Albertine Rift floor. The altitudinal range is 670-760 m (Howard 1991). It is drained by three main streams.

Nyahuka and Rwigo streams drain west into rivers Lamia and Tokwe and eventually into Semliki, while Kirumia stream drains north directly into river Semliki (Langdale-Brown *et al.* 1964). The landscape is underlain by rocks of old lake deposits and basement complex granites. Soils are rift valley sediments, grey alluvial clay soils that tend to be alkaline and of poor fertility. The wettest months in the park are March to May, and September to December, with average annual rainfall of 1,250mm. Annual mean temperature ranges from 18°C minimum to 30°C maximum.

3.5.2. Biological Environment

The park is considered an easterly extension of DRC's extensive Ituri Forest as its flora and fauna show a strong resemblance to the Congo Basin species (Howard 1991). The forest is classified as moist semi-deciduous and is dominated by the Ironwood tree, *Cynometra alexandrii*. Seven percent of the park is swamp forest dominated by *Mitragyna rubrostipulosa*, the palm *Elaeis guineensis*, and the fig *Ficus vogeliana* (Langdale-Brown *et al.*1964 –figure 7).

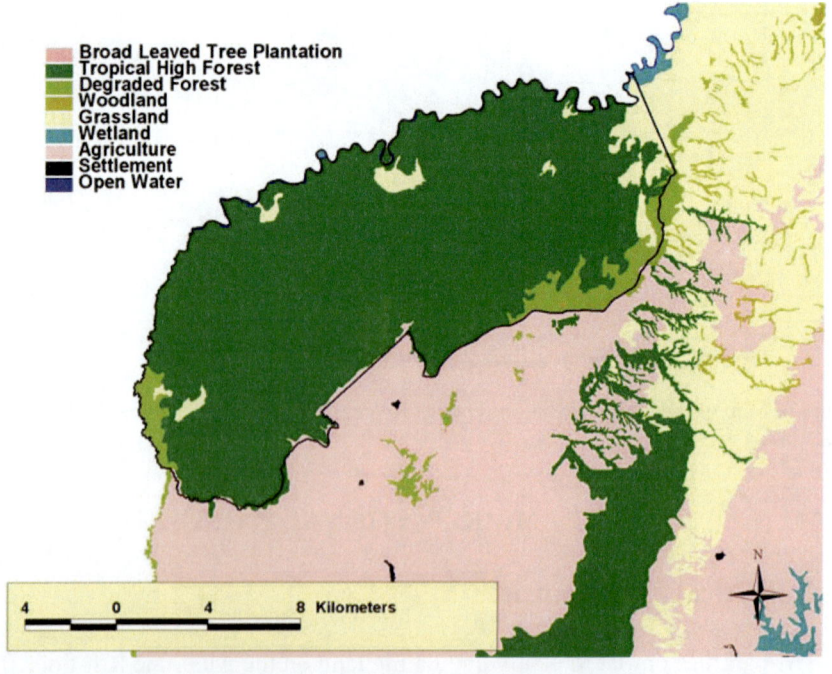

Figure 7. Map of the main vegetation types in and around Semliki National Park.

It is a biologically rich area and was part of the Pleistocene refugium. The area supports fauna characteristic of the 'Guinea-Congolian' and the 'Lake Victoria Regional Mosaic' centres of endemism in Africa.

The park has at least 331 tree species with six species only found in this forest, although common in DRC (Forest Department, 1996e). At least 441 bird species have been recorded here, of which 2 are restricted range species. The park has at least 86 mammal species of which 9 species or subspecies are threatened (Plumptre *et al.* 2003b). Bates pygmy antelope *Neotragus batesi* is only found in this park in East Africa, and the park is also particularly important for its populations of mona monkeys (*Cercopithecus pogonias denti*), found no where else in Uganda and de Brazza monkeys (*Cercopithecus neglectus*) which is also found on the lower slopes of Mt. Kadam, Mt. Elgon, and a few isolated localities of the country (Struhsaker 1981a). Large mammals include elephant, forest buffalo, hippo, leopard and the chimpanzee (currently about 50 individuals, Plumptre *et al* 2003a). With eight species of diurnal primate in Semliki and nine in Kibale these are the two richest forests in East Africa for Primates. Given the instability in the DRC, this area is especially important for conservation of species whose range is limited to this part of East Africa and the Congo Basin.

3.6. MT ELGON NATIONAL PARK

3.6.1. Physical Environment

The most prominent feature of the park is the mountain itself, which is an extinct shield volcano with gentle slopes measuring 3-4°. The lower part of the mountain is made up of a series of benches separated by prominent cliffs, a product of differential weathering of various volcanic materials. The combined action of weathering and salt mining by humans and animals have created numerous caves in the park, some of which are 300 m or more in length (UWA 2000b). On the Kenya side these caves are visited by elephants which mine them for salts and may have contributed to their creation.

Volcanic action on Mt Elgon is dated to early Miocene times, 10-25 million years ago. The rock is comprised of tuff, coarse agglomerates, basalts and mudflow materials. The base of Mt Elgon is larger than that of Mt Kilimanjaro, leading to the thinking that at one time it was higher than the latter. A major eruption in the past is believed to have collapsed volcanic material back into the crater, resulting in the formation of an enormous caldera, 8 km in diameter, one of the largest craters in the world. The soils are brown to red-clay loams below

3,000m, up to a metre or more deep, and shallow black humus soils above 3,000m. Being of volcanic origin, the soils are relatively young and fertile, and are high in calcium, sodium, and potassium (UWA 2000b).

Rainfall is determined by the relief and proximity to Lake Victoria and is higher on the southern and western slopes than northern and eastern slopes. It occurs throughout the year with drier periods between July-August and December-February. The park receives 1,500 to 2,500 mm per year (Howard 1991). Mid-slope locations at elevations between 2,000 and 3,000 m tend to receive more rainfall than the lower slopes or the summit (UWA 2000b). Mt Elgon is probably Uganda's best example of the role of parks as water catchments. The park is drained by an extensive river system that supplies water to several major towns in eastern Uganda and is important for the agriculture, fisheries, and livestock industries in the region. Tororo, Mbale, Kapchorwa, and Bukwo towns obtain their water from rivers draining out of the park. There are four main rivers and river systems, a) to the northeast, River Suam drains along the Uganda/Kenya border into Kenya, while River Bukwa drains through Bukwa town, emptying into River Suam on the Kenyan side of the border, b) to the northwest are rivers Nyenye and Sipi that flow into the Lake Okolitorom swamp system in Nakapiripirit district. Rivers Muyembe, Namusenene, Sironko, Simu, and Gwaragu drain into Lake Opeta swamps in Teso. Waters of the northwestern rivers eventually drain into Lake Kyoga through Lake Bisina, c) to the southwest, River Manafwa flows into the Mpologoma swamps, and d) to the south, River Lwakhaka flows southwards along the Uganda/Kenya border before its confluence in Busia District with River Malaba from Kenya and draining through the Kibimba swamps into the Mpologoma River.

3.6.2. Biological Environment

Like other mountains in Uganda the vegetation consists of different belts of plant associations found at different altitudes (figure 8). The park has the following four major vegetation types: a) mixed montane *Juniperus-Podocarpus* forest (up to 2500m) (48% of the park area), b) bamboo and low canopy montane forest (2400-3000m) (21% of the park area), c) high montane heath (3000-3500m) (7% of the park area), and d) moorland (>3500m) 24% of the park area (UWA 2000b). The high altitude moorland and heath zone is rich in species endemic to Mt Elgon or shared with other EA mountains. It is home to four regional endemics; a subspecies of the white-starred forest robin (*Pogonocichla stellata elgonensis*), the four striped grass mouse (*Rhabdomys pumilia*), the three spot sylph butterfly *Metisella trisignatus*, and the moth *Imbrasia krucki* (Byaruhanga *et al.* 2001). The vegetation of Mt Elgon NP has at least 273 tree and shrub species.

The park has recorded 23 mammal species, most of the larger ones having been hunted to extinction. Three large mammal species; the bongo *Tragelaphus eurycerus*, buffalo *Syncerus. caffer*, and giant forest hog *Hylochoerus meinertzhageni* previously recorded in the forest are extinct on the Ugandan side of the mountain, while elephants may only visit the forest occasionally from the Kenyan side of the mountain. The park has 296 bird species and in Uganda, it is the only park with Jackson's francolin, bronze-naped pigeon, Hartlaub's turaco, and tacazze sunbird that are endemic to the East African Mountains. In addition, races of a number of bird species are restricted to this mountain (UWA 2000a).

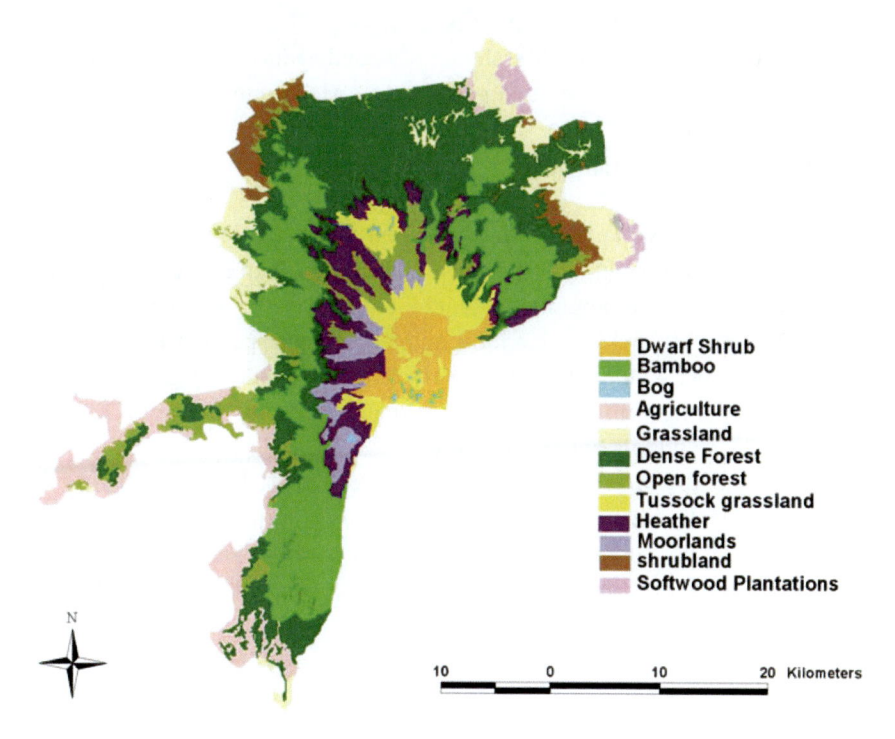

Figure 8. Map of the main vegetation types in Mt Elgon National Park.

3.7. BUDONGO CENTRAL FOREST RESERVE

3.7.1. Physical Environment

The forest is bisected by rivers Sonso, Waisoke, Wake and Bubwa which drain into Lake Albert (Forest Department, 2002). Outside the forest reserve, there are numerous lengthy riverine forests to the south and southwest forming arms of the forest that stretch out into the surrounding areas (Reynolds 2005). The forest lies between 700 m and 1,270 m (Forest Department, 2002). The underlying Precambrian rocks predate the formation of the western rift valley during the tertiary. Soils are red and vary from heavy loam/sandy clay to a very sandy loam (cited in Sheppard 2000). Rainfall varies between 1,240 mm and 2,187 mm per annum with a mean of 1,600 mm. It is bimodally distributed through the year, with most rain falling between March and May and again between September and November. Temperatures are generally even. Mean monthly maximum and minimum temperatures average 32°C and 19°C.

3.7.2. Biological Environment

Budongo forest supports a variety of forest types (figure 9). Broadly, 53% is forested while 47% including most of the Kaniyo-Pabidi and Kitigo blocks comprises grassland communities thought to be capable of supporting forest (Howard 1991). The forest has the most number of tree species (449) recorded for any Ugandan forest. In the 1940s, the reserve was surrounded by grassland but the forest was expanding with a mixture of tree species, notably *Maesopsis* colonizing grassland areas around its border.

At that time, the forest consisted of four forest types, 1) the colonizing forest at the edges which was of two types, the *Maesopsis* forest on rich soils and the woodland forest on poorer soils; 2)The mixed forest which was rich in tree species, including the mahoganies (*Khaya anthotheca* and three species of *Entandrophragma*) and at least 50 species reaching the canopy; 3) Ironwood Forest, with *Cynometra* occurring at all sizes and a general paucity of other species; and 4) Swamp Forest occurring along seasonal rivers which contained *Calamus* (rattan climber), wild palms (*Raphia farinifera*) and riverine tree species such as *Pseudospondias microcarpa* and *Mitragyna stipulosa*. Today, following intensive management of the forest for timber production, the vegetation in the reserve closely resembles that described by Eggeling (1947).

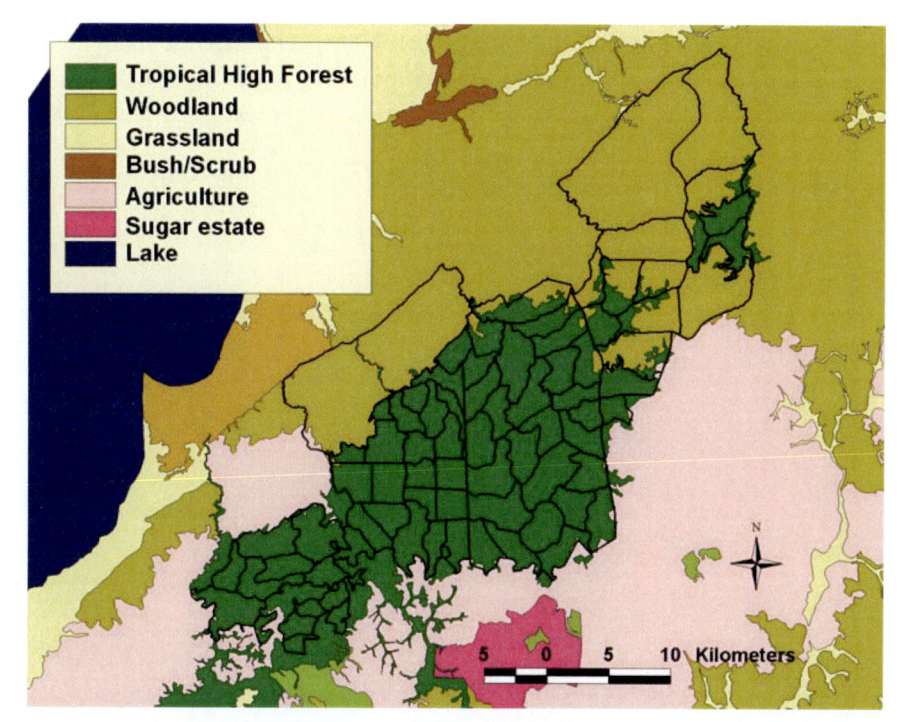

Figure 9. Map of the main vegetation types in and around Budongo Forest Reserve. The map also shows the locations of the different logging compartments in the forest.

The main differences are that some of the surrounding grasslands outside the Reserve have been replaced by crops, *Cynometra* forest is much reduced, and mixed forest is much expanded with fewer mature mahoganies and a higher abundance of fig trees (Reynolds, 2005; Plumptre 1996). The forest has 32 tree species found in no other Ugandan forest (Forest Department 2002).

The reserve is generally poor in primate species, being furthest from DR Congo and the Pleistocene refugium (Reynolds 2005).

Budongo's fauna consist of a population of about 580 chimpanzees (Plumptre *et al.* 2003a), four monkey species: redtail monkeys, *Cercopithecus ascanius*, blue monkeys, *C. mitis*, black-and-white colobus monkeys, *Colobus guereza*, and baboons, *Papio anubis*, and two prosimians, *Perodicticus potto* and *Galago galagoides*. Other mammals include blue duiker, Weyn's duiker, bushbuck, bushpigs, red river hogs, porcupines, honey badgers, and elephant shrews. Although elephants used to be abundant in the forest in the past, none are found there today, the last having been eliminated during the 1981-86 civil war. The reserve has 362 bird species, including the endangered Nahan's francolin. 95

species of mammal, 289 butterfly species, and 130 species of large moth are also found in the reserve (Forest Department 1996c). The forest has 4 bird, 4 moth, and 2 butterfly species not found elsewhere in Uganda (Forest Department 2002).

Chapter 4

BIOLOGY AND BEHAVIOR

Prescribing management interventions for species in the face of new or changing threats requires understanding of their ecological requirements, natural behaviours, population trends and distribution, and factors influencing them. As a result, knowing the behaviour of individual species can be useful for designing management actions. By understanding animal social systems and dispersal patterns, as well as their food habits, we can try to predict the outcome of habitat disturbance (e.g. by timber harvesting or un-prescribed resource extraction or burning) or changes in climate.

This section reviews the published information on the behaviour of most visible species in forests (e.g. primates and elephants) and those known to have profound ecological roles (e.g., fig trees that fruit in all seasons, sustaining frugivores through low-fruit seasons); and predators that help to keep animal population sizes at or below habitat carrying capacity.

The section also deals with species interactions and their roles in the ecosystem. Some species can dramatically impact the environment when they change in abundance for examples changes in elephant numbers in many forests over time has had impact on seed dispersal, tree regeneration and tree abundance. Lastly, this chapter presents evidence on mechanisms thought to regulate wild populations. Understanding these mechanisms is necessary for developing solutions to population declines.

4.1. BASIC BIOLOGY AND BEHAVIOUR OF KEY TAXA

4.1.1. Mammals

Primates

Primates are probably the most visible and best studied of all animals in forest habitats. They are important seed dispersers. Primate viewing, along with mountain climbing, is currently a major tourism attraction in Uganda's forest parks. The majority of the primate species in Ugandan forests are diurnal and only the bushbabies and the potto are nocturnal. Some species such as the gorilla, chimpanzee, olive baboon, and l'hoest monkey usually travel on the ground but frequently feed in trees. The rest of the forest monkeys forage and travel predominantly in trees, but sometimes come to the ground. Most of the primates in Uganda are found in forests. Only one, the patas monkey, is found exclusively in savanna grassland and woodland (Table 2). Most of the studies on primates in Uganda have focused on chimpanzees, gorillas, various monkey species in Kibale and Budongo, and golden monkeys in Mgahinga.

Table 2. Primate species in Ugandan parks and Budongo Forest Reserve. With exception of the patas monkey, *Erythrocebus patas* which is found exclusively in the savannas of MFNP and KVNP, all of Uganda's 20 primate species occur in forest parks. Other primates (diurnal species only) found in savanna parks are chimpanzees (QENP and Rabongo forest of MFNP) baboons (all the four savanna parks- QENP, MFNP, KVNP, LMNP), Black-and-White colobus (MFNP, QENP) vervet monkeys (all the four parks), the blue monkey (Maramagambo forest of QENP, Strips of forest in KVNP), L'hoest's monkey (Maramagambo forest of QENP) and the redtail monkey (QENP, MFNP)

	Common name	Scientific name	Forest found
1	Black-and-White Colobus	*Colobus guereza*	All forests except Mgahinga
2	Red Colobus monkey	*Procolobus badius*	Kibale
3	Rwenzori colobus	*Colobus angolensis*	Rwenzori
4	Blue monkey	*Cercopithecus mitis stuhlmanii*	All forests except Mgahinga, Mt Elgon
5	Golden monkey	*Cercopithecus mitis kandti*	Mgahinga
6	Redtail monkey	*Cercopithecus ascanius*	Budongo, Kibale, Rwenzori, Semliki, Bwindi
7	L'Hoesti monkey	*Cercopithecus l'hoesti*	Kibale, Bwindi, Rwenzori

Table 2. (Continued)

	Common name	Scientific name	Forest found
8	Vervet monkeys	*Cercopithecus aethiops*	Kibale, Semliki
9	Gray-Cheeked Mangabey	*Lophocebus albigena*	Kibale, Semliki
10	Olive baboon	*Papio anubis*	Bwindi, Kibale, Semliki, Budongo, Mt Elgon
11	Eastern chimpanzee	*Pan troglodytes schweinfurthii*	Kibale, Budongo, Semliki, Rwenzori, and Bwindi
12	Mountain gorilla	*Gorilla beringei beringei*	Bwindi, Mgahinga
13	De Brazza monkey	*Cercopithecus neglectus*	Semliki, Used to occur in Mt Elgon but status unknown
14	Mona monkey	*Cercopithecus mona*	Semliki
15	Eastern needle-clawed galago /Spectacled galago	*Galago matschiei*	Bwindi, Kibale, Ruwenzori? Semliki? Mgahinga?
16	Senegal galago	*Galago senegalensis*	Mt Elgon
17	Dwarf galago	*Galago thomasi*	Kibale, Bwindi, Semliki
18	Demidoff's galago	*Galago demidoff*	Kibale, Bwindi, Semliki
19	Potto	*Perodicticus potto*	Kibale, Budongo, Bwindi, Semliki, Rwenzori?

Sources: Struhsaker (1997), Kingdon (1974), UWA management plans, Reynolds (2005). The distribution of galagos and pottos (nocturnal primates) is less certain than that of the diurnal primates. Protected Areas with a question mark may have them, according to the description by Ambrose.

Socio-Ecology

Apes

The sociology and ecology of Ugandan apes is among the best-understood in the world. Chimpanzees live in loose groups called "communities" which may consist of up to 150 members, from which chimpanzee males from other communities are excluded. The Kanyawara and Ngogo communities in Kibale number 52 and 145 individuals respectively (Santiago *et al.* 2003), while the Sonso community at Budongo now has about 74 individuals (Reynolds pers. comm.).

Gorillas, the other ape species in Uganda, live in groups rarely exceeding 20 individuals (3-25 in Bwindi in 1997, McNeilage *et al.* 1998) and dominated by one or two Silverback males. Chimpanzees and gorillas make nests either to rest in during the day, or to sleep in at night. Gorillas usually nest on the ground or in low woody shrubs. At Budongo, male chimpanzees nest lower than females (Brownlow *et al.* 2001). Other interesting behaviors include drumming and vocalization. While gorillas chest-beat, chimpanzees beat tree buttresses and tend to be more vocal. One of the commonest calls they make is the pant-hoot, commonly made by adult males arriving at fruiting trees. These calls were previously thought to inform other chimps about large food patches and to attract them to the patches. More recent studies have shown that arrival pant hoots serve to mark the status of the individuals making them (Clark and Wrangham 1994).

Both chimpanzees and gorillas are more genetically similar to human beings than any other living organism, and chimpanzees are closer to humans than are gorillas (Ruvolo 1997, Wimmer *et al.* 2002). The extent of similarity is still under debate. Wildman *et al.* (2003) have estimated that humans share 99.4% of functional DNA with chimpanzees, but some studies have put the estimate as low as 95% (Britten 2002). Despite morphological evidence to the contrary (Sarmiento *et al.* 1996), DNA evidence suggests that Bwindi and Mgahinga gorillas are not genetically distinguishable and probably belong to the same subspecies (Garner and Ryder 1996).

Human beings and chimpanzees also share a unique social structure. Chimpanzee females, like human females commence reproduction at the age of 10-15 years (Wallis 1997) and like human societies which are 'hunter gatherers', chimpanzee communities are fluid, with parties constantly breaking up and reforming. This "fusion-fission" form of organization, also occurs to some extent among mangabeys and lions, but is generally rare among social animals. Females are generally reported to have inter-birth intervals of 4.4-6 years (Wrangham *et al.* 1994a, Boesch and Boesch-Achermann 2000) but intervals of 5.2 and 5.7 years have been reported for Sonso (Budongo) and Kanyawara (Kibale) respectively (Thompson *et al.* 2006). In Kibale, chimpanzee community ranges have been estimated at approximately 25-35 km^2, but males use areas 1.5-2 times greater than that used by females. In Budongo, Reynolds and Reynolds (1965) estimated the home range size of the Busingiro community as 15.5-20.7 km^2 for a community of 60-80 chimpanzees and the home range of the 46-member Sonso community was 14.51 km^2 (Newton-Fisher, 2003). In Kibale, females have been recorded to have smaller core areas within the home range that is defended by the males. Gorilla groups on the other hand occupy home ranges of 13km^2 - 34km^2 in Bwindi and 4-20km^2 in the Virunga volcanoes. These differences are believed to be related to the occurrence of fruit which is more abundant at Bwindi than in the Virungas. Gorillas range more widely during fruiting seasons (Nkurunungi 2003).

Another feature of chimpanzees and gorillas, which is rare among other mammals, is female dispersal. When females reach maturity, they emigrate to the territory of a new community to mate. In contrast, males spend their entire lives in the territory where they were born. Female dispersal results in communities where males are closely related, whereas females may or may not be related to one another. Understanding factors shaping chimpanzee socio-ecology may shed light on how human hunting-and-gathering societies evolved (Ghiglieri, 1985).

Like humans, chimpanzees are among a few mammal species that engage in lethal coalitionary aggression between groups (Wrangham and Peterson 1996). Most attacks on neighbours occur when parties, made up mostly of adult males, patrol boundaries of their community's range. Males patrol relatively often with others with whom they associate in grooming and within-community coalitions (Watts and Mitani 2001). Like humans, chimpanzees engage in intercommunity killing; this has been observed at least three times in Kibale (Muller 2002, Watts *et al.* 2006). Violent intercommunity conflicts have been observed at Budongo as well (Reynolds 2005). Intra-community killings of young males rising through the male dominance ranks have been reported at Ngogo in Kibale (Watts 2004) and in Budongo (Reynolds 2005).

Other Primates

Other primates also show varying demographic and social patterns. Monkey groups have smaller home ranges and have varying levels of cohesiveness. Red colobus in Kibale (figure 10) live in large multi-male social groups numbering approximately 50 individuals. Home ranges average 34 hectares, and those of adjacent social groups overlap extensively. Average adult sex ratios in groups are two females to one male. Red colobus are another of the primates in which females transfer between groups while males stay in their natal groups. Black-and-White Colobus in Kibale live in groups with usually one adult male, 3-5 adult females averaging 10 individuals. Home range size is the smallest observed for any Ugandan monkey, averaging only 16 hectares (Oates 1977a, Plumptre *et al.* 1997a). Males transfer between groups, while females remain resident.

In Kibale, Gray-cheeked mangabeys live in groups averaging 15 individuals, but the groups vary in size from six to 30 individuals. Uganda mangabeys are currently a subject of review and may be a new species, *Lophocebus ugandae* (Groves 2007). Home range sizes are usually 100-400 ha (Waser 1977b, Olupot et al. 1994). Large mangabey groups (larger than 18 individuals) tend to break up and re-unite fairly frequently. Each group usually has several males, and up to 10 have been recorded for a group in Kibale (Olupot and Waser 2001a).

The number of mature males in a group appears to be determined by the number of females in estrus. Groups are female bonded, with males showing a tendency to leave their groups as individuals, while female dispersal rates are not yet known (Olupot and Waser 2005).

Figure 10. Male Red Colobus monkey in Kibale National park. A large percentage of the population of this species is killed by chimpanzees each year (A.Plumptre/WCS)

Blue monkeys are more widely distributed than red colobus and mangabeys, occurring in all the forests reviewed here. They live in one-male groups but seasonal incursions of extragroup males into groups does occur. In Kibale, the groups average 25 individuals and their home ranges approximate 60 hectares. Within groups, there are approximately 10 adult females, and males move between groups while females usually stay in their natal groups. In Budongo, groups have on average four adult females and group size averages 10-12. Home range sizes range from 8 to 19 ha (Fairgrieve 1995). In Mgahinga, golden monkey groups have 2-62 individuals and average 30 individuals (Twinomugisha *et al.* 2003). Golden monkeys are currently considered a subspecies of blue monkeys though may be a separate species.

Redtail monkeys live predominantly in one-male groups, averaging 30 individuals in Kibale. It is mainly the males that disperse. Home range sizes are approximately 24 hectares. In Budongo, they are found in smaller overlapping home ranges in logged forest, whereas groups in unlogged forest, where their density is 4 times lower, do not have overlapping home ranges (Sheppard 2000, cited by Reynolds 2005). In Kibale, the ratio of adult males to adult females in the groups averages 1:9.

Feeding Ecology and Diet

Based on their diets, forest primates can be classified into four broad groups: fruit eaters (frugivores); leaf, bark, and pith eaters (folivores); gum eaters (gummivores); and species that take substantial quantities from more than one of these food classes, often including insect and to some extent vertebrate prey (omnivores).

Among primates classified as frugivores, chimpanzees are the most frugivorous of all (figure 11). In the Kanyawara area of Kibale Forest, fruit accounts for 60-72% (Isabirye-Basuta 1989, Wrangham *et al.* 1991) of the chimp diet in most cases and fruit eating may take up to 81% of their feeding time (Pebsworth *et al.* 2006). In Budongo, fruit and seeds take up 79% of feeding time (Pebsworth *et al.* 2006, Plumptre 2006). Frugivores preferentially take ripe fruit over unripe ones, and their preferences for ripe over unripe fruits can be explained in respect to both nutrients and secondary compounds such as condensed tannins (Wrangham and Waterman 1983), but chimps generally select food according to the sugar concentration more than tannin levels (Reynolds *et al.* 1998, Reynolds 2005).

Size of a foraging party is strongly influenced by the amount of fruit in a particular tree. As the crown volume of a fruiting tree increases, so does the maximum number of apes observed foraging in the tree (Ghiglieri 1985). However, a fibrous diet of tree leaves (generally young) is also taken from species such as *Celtis africana*, *C. durandii*, and *Ficus exasperata* (Isabirye-Basuta 1990, Wrangham *et al.* 1991).

Terrestrial Herbaceous Vegetation (THV) are another fibrous food eaten. Plants such as *Pennisetum purpureum*, *Acanthus pubescens*, *Afromomum mala*, *Marantachloa leucantha*, *Acalypha ornata*, and *Ficus ornata* are the main source of THV. Herbaceous pith from the inside of plant stems is an important food resource, offering an alternative energy supply when fruits are scarce. Chimps in Kibale feed on pith of THV 17.6% of their feeding time (Wrangham et. al. 1991), but pith-feeding by chimps is rare in Budongo. Dense ground vegetation, which covers gaps after forest disturbance has been shown not to contain more edible THV for chimpanzees than forest with more tree cover. THV tends to occur in areas where the soil is waterlogged, but is equally common in the forest understory as in the dense ground vegetation that covers gaps after forest disturbance. For Kibale chimpanzees, a common activity pattern is to eat fruit in the morning, and forage in the forest edge in the latter part of the day, where they find a richer assemblage of THV than in pure forest. Thus the habitat mosaic is important for Kibale chimpanzees that live in areas of low THV densities. Figures indicate the THV levels in Kibale are too low to sustain even one breeding group of gorillas which may be why they never reached here (Wrangham *et al* 1993).

Figure 11. A chimpanzee feeding on figs in Budongo Forest Reserve. Chimpanzees are the most frugivorous of all the primate species in Uganda (A.Plumptre/WCS).

Other than plant material, meat can be an important food item for chimpanzees. When hunting, chimpanzees take mostly arboreal monkeys. In Kibale, chimpanzees mainly hunt red colobus monkeys, and to a lesser extent redtails, blues, and black-and-white colobus. The impact of chimp predation on red colobus is so serious that red colobus density is negatively correlated to chimpanzee density (Plumptre and Cox, 2005). At Budongo where there are no red colobus monkeys, chimpanzees hunt mainly blues, black and white colobus, and redtail monkeys, but have occasionally been observed killing duikers.

Soil and dead wood form a lesser food item. Soil is ingested in an apparent quest for nutritional and dietary supplements and/or pharmaceuticals (Mahaney *et al*. 1997, Reynolds 2005, Tweheyo *et al*. 2006). Analyses of the soil samples have shown that soil eaten is very high in iron, but low in other minerals. Minerals such as calcium, chromium, cobalt, bromine, and iodine are either relatively low or are below their detection limits. Iron may play a role in replenishing haemoglobin which would be important in chimpanzee physiology at the high elevations. However, Metahalloysite, a partially hydrated clay mineral that acts much like the pharmaceutical Kaopectate™ is the most likely mineral stimulus. Pharmaceutical Kaopectate™ is used to alleviate the effects of diarrhoea in humans. The clay minerals may act similarly to alleviate the effects of diarrhoea among chimpanzees (Wrangham 1995). Primates are thought to ingest soil for mineral supplementation, adsorption of toxins, treatment of diarrhoea and pH adjustment of the gut (Krishnamani and Mahaney 2000). Sodium seems to be an important nutrient in forests for primates and is one of the few minerals that seems to be in short supply in primate diets. Sodium can be at relatively high concentrations in dry wood which may explain some primates consume this food item (Rothman 2006b).

Not all plant items ingested by primates are nutritive. Chimpanzees appear to regularly ingest young leaves of *Ficus exasperata*, *Rubia cordifolia*, *Aspilia mossambicensis*, and pith of *Vernonia amygdalina* for their medicinal properties. Presumed medicinal compounds in these leaves are furanocoumarins, triterpenes, cyclic oligopeptides, thiarubins, steroidal glycosides, and sesquiterpene lactones respectively (Rodriguez and Wrangham, 1993). The presence of thiarubin A, a powerful antibiotic and anthelmintic diathiane polyine found in the leaves of *Aspilia* has also led to the suggestion that these plants are ingested for the expulsion of parasites (Wrangham and Goodall 1989). In Kibale, tapeworms (*Bertiella studeri*) have been found in chimp dung during periods of elevated swallowing of leaves of *Aneilema aequinoctiale* and *Rubia cordifolia* (Wrangham 1995) and leaves of *A. aequinoctiale* and *Aneilema orientalis* in Budongo (Reynolds 2005). Physical properties of these leaves are also thought to help with parasite expulsion. All the leaves swallowed by chimpanzees are bristly haired, or have a rough surface, in contrast to most leaves where they live which are smooth and not noticeably rough (Huffman and Wrangham 1994; Reynolds 2005). It is however not known why chimpanzees ingest berries rich in secondary compounds (e.g., *Phytolacca dodecandra*) which are a concentrated source of toxic triterpenoid saponins known to be highly fatal to rats, mice, molluscs, and viruses. Of 25 plant species eaten by chimps and also used by local people for medicinal purposes in Budongo and Kibale (Pebsworth *et al.* 2006) eight parts are known to be pharmacologically active. These include flowers of *Acanthus pubescens* which have antibiotic properties; bark of *Alstonia boonei* which is antiprotozoal and antimetazoal compounds; leaves of *Crassocephalum bojeri* and *Trichilia rubescens* which have antimalarial properties; leaves of *Ficus exasperata*, which are antihelmintic, analgesic, antinematodal, and insectidal; leaves of *Chaetacme aristata* which are bacteriostatic; and leaves of *Myrianthus arboreus* which contain triterpene acids.

The next most frugivorous of the forest primates after chimpanzees are the mangabeys. Mangabeys consume fruit approximately 60% of their feeding time. They are omnivores, also spending long periods ingesting young leaf, leaf buds, pith, bark cambium, flowers and flower buds, invertebrate prey, and to a lesser extent soil and vertebrate prey such as snakes. Mangabeys eat substantial quantities of seeds, more so than any other primate, consuming large quantities of seeds of *Diospyros abyssinica*, *Albizia*, *Croton* spp., *Acacia brevispica*, *Pterygota*, and several liana species and other climbing plants (Waser 1977b, Olupot 1998). However, though mangabeys take fruits of *Mimusops*, *Uvariopsis*, *Ficus* species, *Blighia* and others in large quantities, the seeds of these species are discarded under the trees or passed out in dung.

Blue monkeys and redtails are also frugivores, but forage on insects more than mangabeys. Leaf intake varies by site, higher in unlogged forest in Budongo compared with logged forest (Plumptre 2006). Low elevation populations eat more fruit than high elevation ones, which incorporate more leaves and leaf buds in their diet. Golden monkeys at Mgahinga spend more than 50% of their feeding time foraging on bamboo shoots. Bamboo shoots are rich in protein (Twinomugisha 2007). Aside from chimpanzees, only blues have been seen to eat other primates. On the three occasions they have been watched doing so, the victims were bushbabies (Leland and Struhsaker 1987). They also eat other mammals such as flying squirrels in Budongo. In Kibale, R. Rudran (pers. comm.) reported seeing them eat an owl. Redtail diet is very closely related to blues and they often show dietary overlap values above 85% (Plumptre 2006). Of the other guenons, De brazza and mona monkeys have not been studied in Uganda, but elsewhere, they are both known to be omnivores. De brazza's monkeys are known to eat primarily fruit and other items in their diet include leaves, flowers, mushrooms, beetles, termites, and worms. Mona monkeys feed on fruit, leaves, shoots, insects, nuts, grains, roots, wild honey, bird eggs, and snails.

Mountain gorillas, red colobus, and black-and-white-colobus monkeys are primarily folivorous, feeding mainly on leaves, bark, and pith. Mountain gorillas spend approximately 57% of the time feeding on leaves, 22% eating bark, and 10% pith from over 100 plant species. Fruits are consumed from over 11 plant species 6% of the time. Important fruit trees include *Chrysophyllum* sp., *Maesa lanceolata*, *Myrianthus holstii*, and *Olinia usambarensis*. Lesser items include fungi, deadwood, and flowers (Nkurunungi 2003). As with other primates, diets of different groups vary according to composition of the forest within a group's range. In Buhoma, a lower altitude site has a greater diversity of plant species and higher shrub densities than Ruhija, which has a higher density of herbaceous vegetation eaten by gorillas. Hence gorillas in Buhoma have a higher fruit composition in their diet than Gorillas in Ruhija (Nkurunungi *et al.* 2004). Theirs is however a far more diverse diet than that of colobus monkeys. Young leaves, leaf buds, flowers and mature petioles of a wide variety of plant species are the main component of red colobus diet at Kibale (Struhsaker 1978) and leaf constitutes 56%-76% of the food taken (Chapman *et al.* 2002a). In the Kanyawara study area, *Celtis durandii* Engl. And *Markhamia platycalyx* (Bak.) were the two top ranking food tree species of the red colobus in 1974 and 1975. *Markhamia*, petioles and rachises were selected for their crude protein content, which was higher than that of leaf blades, which had higher fibre content. Petioles had the lowest acid detergent fibre and lignin. For *Celtis*, young leaves were selected over mature leaves. Young leaves had the highest crude protein content of the samples analyzed and low fibre content (Baranga 1982).

Black-and-white colobus, or Guerezas, have a simpler diet by comparison, spending half of their feeding time taking mature leaves of one tree species and overall using fewer tree species and plant parts than red colobus monkeys (Oates 1977a) but that might be an effect of the number of groups studied and the number of animals per group (C. Chapman pers. com). Guerezas also occasionally take flowers, floral buds, and fruit (especially at Budongo, these items can form up to 50-60% of the diet- Plumptre 2006). High dependence on a leaf diet necessitates that colobus monkeys cope with the nutritional limitations inherent in folivory. Red colobus get around this problem by selecting young leaves, which have a high protein to fibre ratio and are also more digestible. Gorillas get around the problem of sodium shortage by feeding on dead wood (Rothman 2006b). Black-and-white colobus, which feed on the narrowest range of food items may counteract the problem by choosing food trees. They restrict most of their feeding to species in the lower forest layers and at the forest edge and to non-woody climbers which are deciduous and typical of colonizing situations (Oates 1977a, Lwanga 2006). In Kanyawara, and Budongo they also adopt the strategy of feeding on soil and or water plants in the swamp pools. Analyses of clay eaten found it had more magnesium, iron, and copper than neighboring soils, and water plants were found to have high levels of sodium, iron, manganese, and zinc compared to other items of Guereza diet. Water plant consumption may remedy mineral deficiencies, while clay may be consumed to adsorb plant toxins or to adjust the pH of the fore stomach (Oates 1978).

Galagos and pottos are relatively unstudied in Uganda. Elsewhere, the main diet of the greater galago is gums and/or fruit; it also eats seeds, nectar, millipedes, and insects (Hladik, 1979; Clark, 1985). The lesser galago primarily eats gum, but also eats insects for protein (Bearder and Martin, 1979). Pottos inhabit the canopy of tropical rain forests, sleeping during the day in the leaves and almost never coming down to the ground. Studies of stomach contents (cited in Estes, *The Behavior Guide to African Mammals*, 1991) have shown that the Potto diet consists of about 65% fruit, 21% tree gums and 10% insects. Pottos have also occasionally been known to catch bats and small birds. Their strong jaws enable them to eat fruits and lumps of dried gum that are too tough for other tree-dwellers. The insects they eat tend to have a strong smell, possibly because more palatable insects are snatched up by faster-moving creatures.

Forest dwelling baboons are among the least studied diurnal primates in Uganda with so far only two studies conducted at Budongo. Baboons are one of the main sources of conflict between people and parks, often found along the forest edges. They are opportunistic and seize any opportunity to obtain food. Baboon diet cuts across all primate diets, theirs being much less specialized, akin to human, but with a wider variety of food items. Diet composition of baboons varies remarkably across habitats. For example the diet of baboons at Sonso and Busingiro in Budongo overlap by only 4 plant species out of a total of 58 forest plant species eaten yet the two areas are about 8km apart (Paterson 2006). Forest baboons living away from the forest edge at Budongo (Sonso) eat mainly leaves (17% of feeding time); fruit and seed (47% of feeding time); stem, bark, and roots (17% of feeding time), and garbage from the camp (17% of the time) (Okecha and Newton-Fisher 2006). *Broussonetia papyrifera*, an exotic tree planted experimentally in a clearing at Sonso was the most consumed species, and fruits and leaves were taken. Baboons also eat gum (from Khaya bark) insects, and soil (Paterson 2006). At Sonso, baboons may ingest 10 different food plant species within 30 minutes and different species may be ingested within one minute. At other times, intensive feeding on a food item can last for several hours (*Ibid.*).

Primates sometimes practice cannibalism, often of infants. It is generally thought that infanticides are undertaken by new dominant males that have entered the group to get females back in oestrus so that they can maximize the number of offspring they have. Instances of cannibalism have been observed in redtails, blue monkeys, and chimpanzees. Struhsaker (1977) reported an incident in which a harem redtail male was replaced by a new male from outside the group and the new male proceeded to kill and eat two newborn infants before copulating with several adult females in the group. In Budongo, a male blue monkey killed and ate an infant and three cases of killing and eating of infants have been reported for chimpanzee males in the same forest (Reynolds 2005). The infanticidal attacks on infant chimps were carried out by high-ranking males on offspring of females that mated more with non-community males or with older adolescents from within the community. Killing and eating of chimpanzee infants by male chimpanzees has also been observed at Ngogo (Watts and Mitani 2000).

Polyspecific Associations

Primate species frequently associate with each other and other species. One typical type of association is when two (or more) species are within close spatial proximity, for instance when they feed in the same tree. Another is when one species responds to the calls of another at a distant location. Depending on the species, polyspecific associations can be quite common or rare. Of the Kibale primates, red colobus associate spatially most frequently, whereas black-and-white colobus tend to be loners (Leland and Struhsaker 1987). The presence of distance associations have been confirmed by experimental playbacks of calls. In Kibale, experiments showed that redtails, blue monkeys, turacos, hornbills, eagles, mangabeys, and chimps frequently associate with each other through calls (Hauser and Wrangham 1990). Redtails, blue monkeys and turacos respond to hornbill calls by looking while mangabeys respond to chimp and great blue turaco calls by making their own alarm calls and changing direction of group movement and to hornbill calls by calling back, or occasionally moving towards the location of the call (Hauser and Wrangham, 1990; Olupot et al. 1998). Other associations involving primates have been observed between dung beetles and monkeys, and guinea fowls with monkeys. Dung beetles at Kibale follow monkeys and insectivorous birds follow the dung beetles (Isabirye-Basuta, pers. comm). Crested guineafowls (Gutter pucherani) in the same park associate with frugivorous monkeys on the forest floor, especially L'Hoest's monkeys, but not the folivorous ones (Seavy et al. 2001).

There are several possible explanations for why species associate. According to one theory, species may come together simply by chance. For instance, species may associate because they happen to meet at abundant food sources. This seems to be the case for most Kibale monkeys (Waser 1984, Chapman and Chapman 2000). Food tends to be a meeting point for mangabeys, blues, redtails, and chimps. The second theory is that species associate with each other to deter predator attacks. The basic premise of this theory is that the more individuals there are congregating, the more eyes there are on alert. Evidence for this is that red colobus and redtails have been observed to associate commonly with each other, and no other explanation for this behaviour seems realistic other than that it is a means of reducing the probability of predation by eagles and chimpanzees (Struhsaker 1981b). Observations show that red Colobus, more than any other monkey species, reduce vigilance when in polyspecific associations (Chapman and Chapman 1996). They also form these associations more often where chimpanzees are in high density and when there are more infants in their groups, suggesting that they may be benefiting most from the antipredator benefits of association (Chapman and Chapman 2000). The third theory is that associations may help with food finding. Current evidence partially supports all three theories (Waser 1980, Chapman and Chapman 2000, Struhsaker 1981b). Kibale monkeys are often found together foraging for insects and the large number of individuals moving together helps to flush insects.

Elephants

Elephants *Loxodonta africana* are conspicuous in forests by their signs but are rarely seen in a forest environment. They are important seed dispersers and their breaking and trampling of vegetation maintains forests in mosaic states necessary for conservation of a wide range of species. They occur in most of Uganda's forest parks, but were eliminated from Budongo forest reserve during the early 1980s and have not been seen in Mt Elgon for many years. Studies of forest elephants have been conducted in Kibale and Bwindi parks which contain the largest populations in forests in Uganda. The Kibale population is the larger of the two, consisting of 390 elephants (Wanyama 2005). The Bwindi population is far smaller, with only about 20-30 elephants in total (Babaasa 1994). Elephants on Mgahinga, Rwenzori, and Semliki national parks move between these parks and adjacent protected areas in neighboring countries. Elephants were more numerous in all the forest parks prior to the 1970s but declined through the years as a result of insecurity and poaching. In Kibale, for instance, Wing and Buss estimated this population to have been about 413 elephants in the late 1960s. The Kibale population is a remnant of a larger population that prior to 1962, migrated between Kibale and Queen Elizabeth National Park or to the Rwenzori Mountains and the DRC during the December-February dry seasons. The current population now inhabiting Kibale may include the nucleus that always stayed in the forest, frequenting the swamps and major watercourses.

Studies of forest-dwelling elephants have mainly focussed on their feeding ecology and ranging behaviour. Ranging patterns are not consistent throughout the years. For example, Wing and Buss (1970) observed that Kibale elephants spent most of their time in the central and southern parts of the park, only visiting the northern areas at the beginning of the wet seasons. At this time, north Kibale was being logged and human activity was high. Observations in the late 1990s suggested that they spent more time north of Kibale during that period (Cochrane 2001). Bwindi elephants range widely in the park during the wet season, feeding more on the bamboo in the high elevation southeastern part of the park when it is producing shoots. At this time they tend to raid crops in the villages adjacent to the park. In the dry season, water is scarcer, and elephants spend most of their time in the vicinity of Mubwindi Swamp (Baabasa 2000). In Kibale, elephants have been reported to utilize nearly every species of woody plant they come across in the forest; some woody species are sought more than others. Elephants browse most on large tree species, especially on individuals of small size classes (<5 cm dbh). In Bwindi, elephants selected *Arundinaria alpina*, *Alangium chinense*, *Polyscias fulva* and *Triumphetta macrophylla*, but opportunistically used 74 other plant species (Babaasa 2000).

Elephant activity plays a profound ecological role in the forests. Elephant's preference for colonizing forest means that they seek out gaps, retarding gap regeneration, and also push over trees, creating new gaps. This is particularly the case for areas visited frequently and browsed intensively. In Kibale, elephant grazing maintains grasslands and gaps in logged areas. Drastic reduction of elephants would probably cause Kibale grasslands to fully revert to forest. This, if it happened, would cause a decline or total loss of grassland associated herbivores. The current population of elephants in Kibale may be suppressing the regeneration of trees in formerly logged areas (Lawes and Chapman 2006). Elephant activity helps to keep the vegetation in a state of flux, maintaining the diversity of habitats and niches for the organisms living in the forest. Such is not the case for Budongo, where research at a time when 500-600 elephants were killed showed that scarring of trees and selective feeding on certain tree species may be the cause of reduced tree diversity in parts of the forest and may have contributed to the monodominance of *Cynometra alexandri* in the forest (Laws *et al.* 1975, Sheil and Salim 2004). This tree has very flaky and very hard bark and consequently is not often eaten by elephants and when it is it doesn't kill the tree, unlike other tree species in the forest.

Deposition and distribution of approximately 45 kg of droppings per animal per day by each elephant has profound impacts on the environment (Wing and Buss 1970). The droppings and vegetation trampled by elephants serve as fertilizer and trampled vegetation helps develop a protective mat of litter that protects the soil, reduces runoff and leaching, and builds up a soil fauna conducive to a richer biotic community. The feeding behaviour and digestive processes of elephants can be particularly valuable where the soils are lateritic, as is the case in many parts of East Africa. Studies in Zimbabwe [Mitchell (1961), cited by Wing and Buss (1970)] have shown that when elephants and other large mammals were destroyed, forests disappeared, land became parched, and the rich biotic community disappeared. However where populations exceeded their forage supply, especially where migratory routes were blocked, the digestive processes and feeding habits destroy the environment as observed in Murchison Falls National Park (see Savannas book). As an integral component of the ecosystem therefore, the elephant population with its feeding behaviour appears to be a key factor in determining total productivity of the parks. Too many elephants and too few elephants can each cause problems.

Carnivores

Carnivores can be considered an indicator species as most require large ranges and decline if their prey species are hunted intensively. As a result, they occur in relatively low densities compared with non-carnivore species. We are aware of only one study of forest carnivores in forest environments (Andama 2000) in Bwindi. Carnivores found in Bwindi included canids (Side-striped jackal *Canis adustus*), civets (African civet *Viverra civetta* and Palm civet *Nandinia binotata*), cat species (Serval *Felis serval*, Wild cat *Felis sylvestris*, and Golden cat *Profelis aurata*), mongoose species (Water mongoose *Herpestes paludinosus*, Slender mongoose *Herpestes sangineus*, Egyptian mongoose *Herpestes ichneumon*, and banded mongoose *Mungos mungo*); genet species (Small-spotted genet *Genetta genetta* and Large-spotted genet *Genetta tigrina*), Honey badger/Ratel *Mellivora capensis*, Otters (Clawless Otter *Aonynx capensis* and Spotted-necked Otter *Lutra maculicollis*) and Zorilla *Ictonyx striatus*. Carnivore species with a wide distribution within Bwindi included the Palm Civet, Serval, Wild Cat, Golden Cat, Genets and Slender Mongoose. Species limited to forest ecotones and degraded habitats included Side-Striped Jackal, African Civet, Zorilla, and Egyptian mongoose. Species restricted to the forest interior included honey badger, clawless otter and spotted-necked otter, populations of which probably decline with habitat degradation and could become prone to extinction with increased habitat disturbance (Andama 2000).

Bush Pigs

Bush pigs are conspicuous in a forest environment because of their large body size, ecological role as seed predators/dispersers and possible facilitators of seed germination and their interactions with man. Bush pigs (*Potamochoerus larvatus*) are little studied in Uganda's protected areas, but their crop raiding patterns have been studied in greater detail. Only one limited study, by Ghiglieri *et al.* (1982) in Kibale has looked at bush pig biology.

Ghighlieri and colleagues found that bush pig group size ranged from 1-11 pigs, with a mean of 3.2. Their feeding behaviour included foraging in creek beds by moving large boulders and eating the organisms found beneath. They were also observed to feed upon the fallen fruits of *Balanites wilsoniana*, *Crysophyllum sp.*,

Cordia, Mimusops bagshawei, and *Parinari excelsa.* Bushpigs, rodents and squirrels are serious predators on seeds. In some instances, however, bush pigs can act as seed dispersers. On at least two occasions, bush pig faeces containing the skin of ripe fruit, and both intact and crushed seeds of *C. albidum* was found by one of the authors.

It was also found that the pigs exhibited at least four pelage colour morphs. Two predominant morphs resembled the western subspecies, *Potamochoerus porcus porcus,* and eastern/southern subspecies, *P. p. koiropotamus.* Kibale forest may be a zone of secondary contact between the subspecies or the Kibale population is intermediate between clinal extremes. Pelage colour morphs found in Kibale are i) rufous (reddish chestnut body with white or off-white facial markings usually extending down the neck mane and dorsal crest to the sacral region), ii) Dark (dark brown to slately-grey to charcoal black body with white to dirty buff facial markings extending down the neck mane to the dorsal crest with two or more color morphs), iii) Blond (tan to light brown body with whitish facial markings sometimes extending to the neck mane and along the dorsal crest to the sacral region), iv) Two-tone (Bright rufous on approximately half of the body and dark brown to black on the other half (ventral and/or anterior) sometimes with white facial markings. A few individuals appear blotchy on a large scale.

4.1.2. Birds

Birds are often ecological indicators because of their tendency to specialize in specific environments and their ability to respond quickly to changing environmental conditions (especially the specialist species). The ecological sensitivity of birds as potential indicators is suggested by their responses to logging, a subject that is discussed later in this book. Studies of the biology and behaviour of forest birds are just beginning.

Pertinent information comes from 9 studies (with widely varying levels of detail): 1) Black-and-white-casqued hornbills (*Bycanistes subcylindricus subquadratus*) in Kibale (Kalina 1988), 2) Crowned eagle *Stephanoaetus coronatus* at Kibale (Struhsaker and Leakey 1990, Mitani *et al.* 2001, and Olupot and Waser 2001), 3) Cassin's Hawk-Eagle *Hieraaetus africanus* at Kibale (Skorupa *et al.* 1984), 4) raptors in Bwindi (Bataamba 1990), 5) Nahan's francolins, *Pternistis nahani* in Budongo (Sande 2001) 6) The handsome francolin *P. nobilis,* in Bwindi (Semmanda 2004), and 7) Stripe-breasted tit *Parus fasciiventer* at Bwindi (Yatuha 2004).

Black-and-White Casqued Hornbills are well known long distance dispersers of rainforest trees. In Kibale, they show a preference for the core of the forest reserve, where there is a high density of trees with >3m circumference at breast height. Fruits comprise about 90% of hornbill diet by volume, with figs comprising 57% of all fruits (Kalina 1988). Hornbill movements are closely related to their diet. During the dry seasons, when fruit is scarce, hornbills travel long distances (up to 6 km) in search of fruiting trees. Seeds from most fruit species are either regurgitated or defecated and dispersed intact. When breeding, female black-and-white-casqued hornbills use mud to seal themselves into a nest cavity after mating, and remain there until a nesting attempt has ended. Naturally formed cavities used are large (<25cm deep) and at a minimum height of 8m above the ground. The male is solely responsible for food provisioning and external defense of the nest. Nest sealing by the black-and-white-Casqued Hornbill appears to function primarily to protect the nest from conspecifics rather than from interspecific predators (Kalina 1988).

Eagles and other forest raptors in general are of conservation concern because of their occurrence at low densities and a requirement for large ranges. Crowned eagles in Kibale prey mainly on monkeys, which form approximately 82-84 % of their prey (Struhsaker and Leakey 1990, Mitani *et al.* 2001) and 2% of the Cercopithecoid primate population in Kibale succumbs to eagle predation every year. Here, eagles have been observed to select prey according to species, age, and sex. Selectivity by age and sex differs between prey species. Among red colobus monkeys, the eagles selected young juveniles and infants, but in four other monkey species they selected adult males. At both Ngogo and Kanyawara, male primates are taken more often than female primates and solitary individuals are more susceptible than individuals in groups. Adults and non-adult primates appear to be killed in numbers roughly equal to their proportional representation in the forest (Mitani *et al.* 2001). Other prey captured by crowned eagles at Kibale include duikers, viverrids, bats, rodents, and hornbills. At Budongo, they primarily ate hyraxes (Andrew Plumptre, pers. obs.).

Cassin's eagle is another of Africa's endangered large raptors. Observations from Kibale suggest that the species breeds annually. Total length of the breeding cycle from hatching to independence was found to be 166-175 days. Eggs are laid during either of the dry seasons (Skorupa *et al.* 1984). Eagles and other raptor species show habitat specialization. In Bwindi, Bataamba (1990) found that four raptor species; the Mountain buzzard (*Buteo oreophilus*), Rufous-chested sparrowhawk (*Accipiter rufiventris*), Harrier hawk (*Polyboroides typus*) and Great sparrow hawk (*Accipiter melanoleucus*) were edge dwellers, whereas crowned eagles used the forest interior more. Crowned eagles fed typically on monkeys, whereas the other species fed upon rodents, which tend to be more abundant near the forest edge.

Forest francolins are large, terrestrial, slow-moving birds. They show adaptations to forest environments and as such can be used as indicators of ecological condition, especially as they are also hunted. In Uganda, Nahan's (*Pternistis nahani*) and the Handsome (*Pternistis nobilis*) francolins are of interest as they are restricted to only a few forests in Uganda (Budongo, Kibale, Semliki, Bugoma, and Mabira), Rwanda, Burundi and the DRC. Nahan's francolin has been studied in greater detail than the Handsome francolin. Nahan's francolins appear to be favored by selective logging. In Budongo, group size averages two individuals but ranges from one to six. Group size is larger in logged than un-logged forest, and the density of groups is higher in logged than un-logged forest. However, francolins bred better in un-logged than logged habitat because the majority of trees with buttresses where francolins preferred to nest were mature (>100cm dbh), and more of these were found in unlogged forest. Roosting takes place between tree buttresses, in areas with little understorey (Sande, 2001). In Bwindi, the effects of timber harvesting on the handsome francolin are not known. The birds are widely distributed in the forest, but occur at highest densities at high elevations in the bamboo zone near Ruhija (Ssemmanda 2004).

The Stripe-breasted tit and Handsome francolin are two of the nearly 40 Albertine Rift endemic bird species (most have not been studied). In Uganda, the Stripe-breasted tit occurs in the Rwenzoris, Bwindi and Echuya at 1,800-3,400 m above sea level. The birds are grey-backed with blackish heads and throats with characteristic blackish stripes down the center of the breast. They inhabit clearings and edges of montane forests and are insectivores. At Ruhija in Bwindi, birds initiated breeding at the onset of the rains and started new clutches in the same nests right after fledging the previous brood. The birds nested in tree holes or dense foliage. Birds at Ruhija preferred to nest on trees in compounds and adjacent to roads implying that they can tolerate some disturbance. *Hagenia abyssinica* trees were preferred for nesting probably because of the characteristic leaf clumps (living or dead) on these trees (Yatuha 2004).

4.1.3. Plants

Not many studies have focused on individual plant species in forest habitat. Only the genus *Ficus* is considered here for its ecological role and relatively large information base.

Figs are a genus of over 750 species of woody trees, shrubs and vines in the family Moraceae (Serrato *et al.* 2004). Found throughout the tropics with a few species extending into the warm temperate zone, 29 species occur in the forests reviewed in this document (Forest Department 1996a-f) with more species in mid-low elevation forests than high elevation forests. Figs play an important ecological role in forests. Ripe fig fruits are eaten by a wide range of frugivorous animals and birds. Because fig trees fruit throughout the year unlike other tree species, figs are an important source of food for forest frugivores during periods of relative fruit scarcity. Fig fruit consumption by forest frugivores is known mainly from studies in Kibale and Budongo. In Kibale, the most important species for frugivores are *Ficus sansibarica (F. brachylepis), F. natalensis, F. saussureana (F. eriobotryoides, F. dawei), F. mucuso, F. sur (F. capensis), F. thonningii,* and *F. stipulifera* and in Budongo *F. sur, F. mucuso, F. exasperata, F. sansibarica, F. natalensis, F. saussureana, F. thonningii, F. polita,* and *Ficus varifolia.*

A fig fruit is derived from a specially adapted flower with individual flowers inside it. The female flowers are pollinated by small wasps that crawl through the opening to lay their eggs inside. The fruit has a bulbous shape with a small opening in the end and a hollow area inside lined with flowers. In many species, both male and female flowers occur within the same fruit. In some species such as *F. carica,* figs occur as two sexes: hermaphrodite caprifigs with both male and female flowers, and figs bearing only female flowers. In such species, fig wasps grow in the caprifigs. When they mature, they mate. The males die-off inside the caprifigs while the females leave in search of immature figs to lay their eggs in. On finding them, they search for suitable female flowers to lay eggs but find none as all styles in these flowers are long compared to those of female flowers inside the caprifigs. As a result, they only pollinate the female flowers but don't lay any eggs until they find the caprifig. There is typically only one species of wasp capable of fertilizing the flowers of each species of fig, and therefore planting fig species outside of their native range results in effectively sterile individuals. Figs can fruit at any time of year and as a result there are usually some in fruit at any moment in these forests. In Budongo, individual trees produce fruit crops from one to five times a year (Tweheyo and Lye 2003).

Fig fruit size varies between species, individuals of the same species, and between fruiting cycles of the same tree. Larger figs have higher water concentrations but still lead to high rates of nutrient intake per minute for chimpanzees, hornbills, monkeys, and turacos (Conklin and Wrangham 1994). Different species have consistent differences in nutrient concentration between the pulp and seed fractions but individuals of the same species can vary widely in the nutrient content of their fruit. Pulp has more water-soluble carbohydrates, complex carbohydrates, calories, and ash while the seeds have more condensed tannins, lipids, and fiber. Studies in Kibale have shown that fig fruits are generally low in protein (*Ibid.*). However, *Ficus exasperata* may be one of the exceptions to this tendency (Kalina 1988). They are also usually low in water soluble carbohydrates, but nevertheless provide an acceptable level of metabolizable energy as up to 70% of the neutral fibre fraction is digested by many medium to large-sized frugivores. Figs are therefore neither high nor low quality food. Fig pulp has a potential nutritional value that one would expect to find in a staple human food item. The strong tendency of frugivores to be attracted to figs appears to be explained by its high metabolizable energy (Conklin and Wrangham 1994).

By attracting animals to where they are located, figs facilitate dispersal of a variety of plant seeds as the visiting animals pass out the seeds in their faeces. One study in Kibale (Waser 1977a) found that the first animals to visit a fruiting fig tree were black-and-white colobus monkeys, barbets, and starlings. As the fruits ripen, the tree was visited by turacos (Great blue and Black-billed), squirrels, and insectivorous birds during the day and at night by bush babies, fruit bats, genets, palm civets, and pottos. Later when the fruit were really ripe, they were visited by chimpanzees. In addition to facilitating seed dispersal, figs also have the property of increasing the soil moisture, and it is also thought that they increase the fertility in their immediate vicinity as feaces are deposited near a fig tree by animals that feed on its fruits, notably primates and other mammals but also birds.

4.1.4. Aquatic Organisms

Aquatic species are widely known as sensitive bio-indicators of natural ecosystems. However, attempts to study aquatic fauna in forest ecosystems are only recent. Available evidence on forest aquatic systems suggest that changes in flood regimes, siltation, sedimentation, removal of overhanging vegetation, and in invertebrate and fish communities can be used as parameters to monitor forest health (Chapman and Chapman 2002c). Changes in light levels and amounts of silt in the water are widely known to be associated with deforestation impacts on aquatic biota. This has also been shown in Bwindi where investigations have shown that biotic community structure is related to water quality (Efitre 2000). Changes in physical and chemical characteristics of river waters in forest parks can also be used as indicators of the health of biotic communities. Little is yet known about species inhabiting forest waters, including their biology and distributions. Forest rivers and swamps might for example be important breeding grounds for fish, providing habitats and food and need to be protected from pollution and degradation by agricultural run-off.

Fish studies have been important in assessing species richness and abundance of fish fauna in Uganda's forests. They are also useful in illuminating habitat preferences of different species, impact of human harvesting and behaviours that may pre-dispose them to overharvesting. Kasangaki (2008) for example found that at least 18 fish species belonging to seven families occur in the Bwindi rivers in quantities that could be harvested by local communities under multiple use agreement with the park. Three species, *Clariallabes* sp, *Amphilius* sp, and *Haplochromis* sp are un-described and therefore new to science.

Kasangaki (2008) also found that river water inside Bwindi (Ihihizo and Ishasha) and outside the park (section of Ishasha River) had different fish fauna. Park fish were larger in body size than fish outside the park. *Barbus altianalis* and *Varicorhinus ruwenzorii* were large-sized fishes found inside the park whereas *Labeo forskalii* and *Mormyrus caschive* were the large sized ones captured outside the park. Park rivers may therefore not only serve as breeding grounds for lake fish, but may also contain unique resident fish populations. In the Rweimbata swamp of Kibale NP, Chapman and Chapman (1994b) documented syncronous air breathing behavior of *Clarias liocephalus*. Groups of fish periodically made rapid synchronous movements to the water surface. Individuals were generally in close proximity to one another, participating in breathing bouts surfacing near the same area in rapid succession. With humans as predators out of the picture, this behaviour is thought to minimize predation risk to each individual. However, it may actually predispose them to capture by humans. Understanding such behaviours makes room for easy assessments of population status. Other studies in Kibale (Chapman and Chapman 2001, Chapman and Chapman 2003, Chapman LJ *et al*. 2004) help understand how forest disturbance can impact the biodiversity of aquatic organisms in forest waters.

4.1.5. Invasive Species

At least three studies have investigated the distribution of exotic species in Uganda's forest parks; Mwima and McNeilage (2003) and Olupot et al. (2009a) in Bwindi and Lejju *et al*. (2001) in MGNP. Species that appear to be spreading on their own in Bwindi are Lantana (*Lantana camara*), which originates from South America; the Mexican cypress (*Cupressus lusitanica*) from Mexico; tea plants (*Thea sinensis*) which are indigenous to India and China; the Rose Gum (*Eucalyptus grandis*) originally from Australia; and the Black Wattle (*Acacia mearnsii*) which is indigenous to Australia, and *Eucalyptus grandis* in MGNP. The Angel's trumpet (*Datura suaveolens*), which originates from South America is also frequent along the edge of Bwindi but it is not clear whether or not it is capable of spreading on its own. Most of what is known about invasive species is typically based on studies conducted elsewhere outside forest environments, yet it is necessary to study these species under local conditions as a preliminary step towards their control. The most visible invaders in these forests are the bracken fern, *Lantana*, and the Black Wattle.

Each leaf of the bracken fern arises directly from a rhizome (horizontal underground stem), and is supported on a rigid leaf stalk. In Bwindi, bracken fern is frequently found on hillsides and slopes. Bracken fern reproduces by spores and vegetatively by rhizomes which are the main carbohydrate and water storage organ. It is a well known invader of gaps and post-fire colonizer in Bwindi. Bwindi elephants frequently dig up and eat the rhizomes. Rhizomes grow under the roots of herbs and tree or shrub seedlings, and when the fronds emerge, they shade the smaller plants. Elsewhere in the world, bracken fern shading on some sites may protect tree seedlings and increase survival, but this has not been observed in Bwindi. Fire benefits bracken by removing competition while it sprouts profusely from surviving rhizomes. New sprouts are more vigorous following fire. It promotes fire by producing a highly flammable layer of dried fronds in during dry periods.

Lantana camara is an ornamental shrub native to tropical America but now occurs in most tropical and subtropical regions of the world. It is not only extremely widespread but it is also generally considered to be a major pest of agricultural and natural areas. *L. camara* is a highly variable species. It may be erect in the open and scrambling in scrubland. Typically, flowers are yellow, later turning orange then red, and remain on the axillary inflorescence for three days. The flowers, when yellow, produce nectar and are pollinated by butterflies and thrips. As this shrub regenerates freely from widely distributed seeds and spreads vegetatively, it rapidly forms extensive, dense and impenetrable thickets in disturbed areas. Disturbance, decreasing competition, and increasing resource availability associated with fire and grazing all promote *Lantana* invasion whereas shading is a limiting factor. Some Lantana populations are somewhat shade-tolerant becoming the dominant understory shrub in open forests (Binggeli 2003). In areas where natural or anthropogenic fires occur they stimulate thicker postfire re-growth. In some regions its large dry biomass increases fire susceptibility and its massive seed production favors rat populations. Allelopathic effects induced by *L. camara* may inhibit growth of other plants and also seed germination of both crops and natural vegetation. In natural areas the shrub has serious deleterious effects on some endemic animal and plant species and is known to displace natural scrub communities as well as prevent natural regeneration of some tree species. *Lantana* forms dense thickets along many tracks and it is reported to be a favorite food source of butterflies. Many of the birds that feed on this plant in other countries tend to be species that occur in secondary habitats and have profited from anthropogenic habitat changes (Binggeli 2003). In Budongo, chimpanzees hide under *Lantana*, possibly to avoid molestation by insects as the leaves and stem have insecticidal properties (Andrew Plumptre pers. comm.). In pasturelands, fire is used to control dense infestations. Regular burning reduces the number of plants.

The Black Wattle (*Acacia mearnsii*) occurs naturally in southeastern Australia. Like other *Acacia* spp., *A. mearnsii* are small trees, evergreen, and 5-10m high. The leaves are dark green, and flowers pale yellow or cream. Mature fruits are dark-brown pods which are a little hairy. Acacias are weak-wooded trees that often split, shed limbs, or fall over (Moore 1998). In some of the countries where it is grown, it has invaded overgrazed and burnt-over pastures, grassland, forest gaps, roadsides and watercourses. Seeds may remain viable in the soil for over 50 years. In Both Bwindi and MGNP, it is found in former croplands and settlements where it was planted for wood, and in Bwindi, it occasionally occurs along edges. Its flowers are a favorite gorilla food in MGNP. *A. mearnsii* spreads by sending up new shoots from lateral roots as well as from seedlings.

In Budongo FR, colonizing forest in the sawmill area is characterized by the paper mulberry tree (*Broussonetia papyrifera*) whereas *Maesopsis eminii* is the dominant colonizer in other areas. Paper Mulberry is an exotic species introduced by the British around the Sonso Sawmill in the 1950s to see if it would grow well there in the hopes that it might provide wood pulp. It failed to grow to the required size but has taken hold in the Sonso forest edge and sawmill clearing. However, it is thought not to be invasive and does not seem to replace other plants in the forest (Reynolds 2005). It is a favorite chimpanzee food. Chimpanzees eat fruits, young leaves and flowers and as a result it ranks fifth among the food preferred by chimps at Sonso (Fawcett 2000 cited in Reynolds 2005).

4.2. PATTERNS OF POPULATION CHANGE AND DISTRIBUTION

We know much less about population numbers of animals living in forest parks than in savanna parks. This is because poor visibility in forest makes it difficult to census forest animals. Indirect methods such as counts of dung frequency have been used to count some species, but these require correction factors to estimate numbers. Ground counts have been made since early 1960s

(Reynolds 1965). These have covered only small areas of the forests or and have often been extrapolated to the rest of the forest which yields questionable population estimates. Recent efforts have standardized the procedures (McNeilage *et al.* 1998, Plumptre *et al.* 2001, Plumptre *et al.* 2003a) that are now being used for assessment and monitoring by UWA, and low cost monitoring is currently being advocated (Olupot and Sheil in review).

4.2.1. Population Change

Little is known about wildlife population sizes in forest parks (Table 3). Density estimates for some species, particularly primates are common in the literature (summarized in Struhsaker 1997, Reynolds 2005, Twinomugisha *et al.* 2006). They are usually from study areas that are small in comparison to the sizes of the parks. For example, a series of censuses indicate that red colobus and blue monkey populations in the Ngogo study area of Kibale are declining (Struhsaker 1997) but it is not known exactly why this is happening. In the same area vegetation enumeration studies have shown that *Parinari excelsa*, which was a dominant tree species in the area, is undergoing poor recruitment and is becoming less dominant (Olupot *et al.* 2004). Tree censuses in 6.57 ha of an old growth forest in the Ngogo study area of Kibale showed slight decreases in species richness (3%), density (8%), and basal area (1.6%) over a period of 23 years (1975-1998) for unknown reasons (Lwanga *et al.* 2000). On the other hand, density of mangabey food trees, including figs increased in the Kanyawara study area between 1972 and 1992 (Olupot *et al.* 1994). While these estimates do not cover entire protected area landscapes, they can be useful for calibration when censusing entire populations.

Gorillas and chimpanzees have seen most frequent study. According to the latest census conducted in 2003/4, Virunga Volcanoes have 380 gorillas; while Bwindi has 300 individuals, according to a census conducted in 2006 (Guschanski *et al.* 2009). Mountain gorillas are capable of increasing at an annual rate of 3-4% (McNeilage *et al.* in press) but population sizes have been growing at a slower rate to this in recent years. Bwindi's population increased from 300 in 1997 to an estimated 320 individuals in 2002 (but see Guschanski *et al.*2009) while Virunga volcano gorillas which numbered about 450 in 1960 decreased to 252 by 1979 and again climbed up to the present number (figure 12).

Estimates of chimpanzee populations indicate that about 5,000 currently occur in Uganda (Plumptre *et al.* 2003a), but this represents the first estimate of chimp numbers in Uganda so trends of population change are less clear.

Table 3. Population estimates of large to medium-sized mammals and diurnal primates in Uganda's forest parks and Budongo forest reserve. Most of the estimates are recent, and mainly from Kibale National Park. The only other estimates available but not listed here for for these categories of mammals are for Blue duikers (640 indiv.) and red duikers (1,280 indiv.) in Budongo Forest (Plumptre _et al._ 2001). n/a = No census results available

	Bwindi Impenetrable NP			Mgahinga GNP		Kibale NP			Rwenzori NP	Semliki NP	Mt. Elgon NP	Budongo FR	
Species	1993/ 1997	2002	2006	1998	2004	1963-70	2001	2005				1992[#]	2000 @
Elephant	20-30*					413[1]	262	393					
Buffalo							124	554	n/a				
Bush pig							410	556					374
Mountain gorilla	298**	320[4]	325-340[5] 297-302[6]		55								
Chimpanzee[2]		213					1,298	921	500	50	n/a	570	580
Baboon								6,468	n/a				
B&W colobus							7,970	7,346				16,900	12,090
Red colobus							32,980	30,218					
Grey-cheeked Mangabey							16,210	11,603					
Golden monkey[3]				3,164-5,059									

Table 3. (Continued)

	Bwindi Impenetrable NP			Mgahinga GNP			Kibale NP		Rwenzori NP	Semliki NP	Mt. Elgon NP	Budongo FR	
Blue monkey												18,900	15,620
L'hoesti monkey							n/a	n/a	n/a				
Rwenzori colobus									n/a				
Redtail							33,460	37,312				14,300	11,910
Mona monkey										n/a			
De Brazza monkey										n/a			

*1993 estimate, **1997 estimate, [#]Plumptre & Reynolds 1994, @Plumptre et al. 2001, [1]from Wing and Buss (1970), [2]Plumptre *et al.* (2003a) [3]Twinomugisha *et al.* (2003), [4]McNeilage *et al.* 2006, [5]McNeilage pers. comm., [6]Guschanski *et al.* 2009, 2001 and 2005 data for non-chimp species at Kibale from Wanyama (2005).

Figure 12. Mountain gorilla numbers have been increasing steadily since the early 1980s as a result of better conservation (A. Plumptre/WCS).

Censuses in Budongo Forest showed little change in chimpanzee numbers in the eight years between 1992 and 2000. Golden monkey censuses in Mgahinga show that this population is stable.Beginning with an estimate of 3.24 groups km^{-2} in 1989, the population increased to 5.11-6.03 in 1998, and then to 3.21-4.28 groups km^{-2} in 2003 (Werikhe 1991, Twinomugisha 2007). Forest-wide trend data are yet to be developed for other taxa.

4.2.2. Population Distribution

Much is known about the distribution of plants and animals on a national and regional scale. Species lists generated for different protected areas help to determine this (e.g. Forest Department, 1996a-f; Eilu *et al*. 2004). This is perhaps best illustrated by primate distribution. We know that black-and-white colobus occur in all the protected areas described here, except Mgahinga, and that blue monkeys occur in all these forests with the exception of Mgahinga and Mt Elgon. We also know that mountain gorillas occur in Bwindi and Mgahinga but not on the Rwenzoris or Mt Elgon, Angolan colobus occurs only on the Rwenzoris (and Sango bay forests), mona monkeys occur only in Semliki, and grey-cheeked mangabeys occur in only in Kibale, Itwara, Semliki, and Bugoma. Budongo and

Bugoma are less than 50 km apart, and are not topographically very different from each other yet have very different abundances and species of primates.

At a regional level, primate species richness has been shown to be correlated with elevation, tree species diversity, forest size, and proximity to the Pleistocene refugia (Struhsaker 1981a, Reed and Bidner 2004) of eastern DRC/western Uganda. Low and medium altitude rainforests are for instance known to be richer than montane forests in primate species (Struhsaker 1981a).

In low and medium altitude forests, primate species richness decreases with a decrease in tree species diversity, and forest size. Forests closer to the two Pleistocene refugia in Eastern DRC, one around Bwindi, and the other lying to the west of the Rwenzoris are richer in the number of anthropoid primates than those further away (*Ibid.*, Table 2).

Within protected areas, species distribution and factors affecting it are relatively better understood for plants than animals. Several publications describe these distributions for entire parks and research sites within protected areas [Howard 1991, Struhsaker 1997 (Kibale), Reynolds 2005 (Budongo), Olupot 2009, Olupot et al. 2009b] although the descriptions are not yet sufficiently detailed. At Kibale, a remote sensing study has reported plant community change, with nearly 17% of the savanna/agriculture community shifting to bushland/woodland class within 14 years (1989-2003- Laporte et al. 2008). Plant distribution at both a regional and protected area level is known to be strongly affected by factors such as elevation, slope, hydrology, soil type, rainfall, geology, and anthropogenic disturbance. Animal population distribution is expected to vary in relation to these variables, but because of logistical difficulties, actual distributions within the PAs are rarely mapped. Continuing improvement of mapping accuracy in forest environments may however eventually make this possible (Nangendo et al. 2007).

Understanding animal distributions within PAs is necessary for the assessment of habitat requirements and the impact of human population pressure. Bwindi gorillas and elephants are not known to use the northern sector of the park, and it is not known why. Elephants are definitely capable of tolerating a wider altitudinal range. Gorillas (eg. in Kahuzi-Biega) are also known to use this whole altitudinal range. Similarly, recent surveys and censuses in the parks show patterns in species distribution (e.g., McNeilage *et al.* 1998, Chapman and Lambert 2000, Plumptre *et al.* 2003a, Wanyama 2005). For example in Kibale, blue monkeys are common in north of the park, but their numbers gradually decline towards the south. Mangabeys are commoner in the south than in the north, and vervet monkeys and baboons occur mostly in the south. Baboons are more abundant in the forest adjacent grasslands, while vervets are more abundant in the extreme south (Chapman and Lambert 2000). Understanding the causes of these distributions will require understanding how these trends change through time, which requires serial data collected over several years.

Other studies have looked at distributions in relation to specific food items, food chemistry and proximity to forest edges. In Budongo, Plumptre (2006) found that black-and-white-colobus densities were correlated with abundance of *Celtis durandii* and blue monkey and redtail numbers in the same forest were correlated with density and percentage of fleshy fruit in the diet (Plumptre *et al.* 1997b). In Kibale, a study by Chapman *et al.* (2002a) suggested that animal distribution is in part determined by food chemistry. The study found that colobus biomass was positively related to mature leaf digestibility with higher biomass where mature leaves were rich in protein but low in fibre. The protein/fibre ratio may one day be used as a basis for manipulating forest regeneration in such a way as to promote a forest that would support high red colobus abundance (Chapman et al. 2008). Food abundance also determines distribution in colobus monkeys. For example, lianas provide a large component of leaves eaten by black-and-white colobus monkeys in Kibale, especially during periods of food scarcity (Oates 1977b). It may be that habitat wide distribution of these monkeys is determined by liana density.

Population distribution has been studied more in Bwindi than other forests. Andama (2000) in his study of carnivores in this forest has shown that scavenging and crop raiding carnivores such as the side-striped jackal (*Canis adustus* Sundevall) and the African Civet (*Viverra civetta* Schreber) are common in the park periphery, where there is high human activity. Non-scavenging carnivores such as the Golden Cat (*Profelis aurata* Temminck) are mostly restricted to sites with minimal human presence. Forest carnivores are not specialized feeders, but feed mostly on rodents and insects. Among the food they eat are wild fruits and food crops. Only the golden cat had a fairly specialized diet, feeding on medium-sized herbivores especially duikers. In Bwindi, monkeys occur in the forest periphery while gorilla groups tend to be in the middle of the forest (McNeilage *et al.* 1998). Olive baboons *P. anubis*, bushpigs *P. larvatus*, and habitutated mountain gorillas *G.b. beringei* frequently use the area within 500m of the edge while other species (the black-fronted and yellow-backed duikers *Cephalophus* spp., the chimpanzee *P. troglodytes* and elephant *L.a. africana*) tend to use the forest interior more (Olupot 2004). Thus, scavenging and crop raiding species that tend to occur at the edges will be threatened by conflict with man. 'Food' animals are threatened by hunting, and species sensitive to forest disturbance are more immediately affected by habitat disturbance at the edge. For plants, early succession tree species such as *Bridelia bridelifolia, Maesa lanceolata, Albizzia gummifera*, *Harungana madagascariensis*, *Polyscias fulva*, and *Macaranga kilimandscharica* are more abundant near the edge than the forest interior, while the reverse is true for late succession species such as *Parinari excelsa* and *Strombosia scheffleri* which either grow poorly in edge conditions, or are more intensely harvested there (Olupot et al. 2009b).

4.3. MECHANISMS OF POPULATION REGULATION

To address the problem of how populations increase and decrease, managers need to distinguish between human-induced population changes and changes as a result of natural causes. The role of consumers (carnivores, raptors, seed predators, seedling predators, browsers, grazers, piscivores) and other environmental factors such as disease and food availability were the natural causes sought for review in this document. Seed dispersers, decomposers and scavengers and pollinators may also play a key role in population regulation in the ecosystem but in less direct ways such as by determining nutrient availability and seed availability. Understanding the diversity of these groups and their roles is key to understanding the causes of some short- and long-term population changes in a protected area. Research is needed on how natural populations are regulated, and on the relative strengths of potential determinants such as food availability, disease agents, climatic factors, small size and isolation of the habitat in which they occur.

In many cases, changes in populations are known, but the underlying causal factors are not. In other cases, the mechanisms are known but their links to population change are not known. For example food availability, predation, parasite infection, and intragroup competition are all thought to regulate Kibale red colobus populations. A study of this has indeed shown increased fecal cortisol levels during times of food shortage and high parasite infection, and that larger groups have high cortisol levels (Chapman *et al.* 2007). However so far, the only indication that high stress leads to population decline is the fact that larger groups have fewer infants per female than smaller groups. Long term population and habitat data are necessary to understand the linkages between population changes and underlying factors.

A few data are available for large mammals and little is known for plants and small bodied mammals. For plants, Lwanga *et al.* (2000) found that tree species richness in Kibale decreased by 3% and species diversity by 8%, while basal area decreased from 49.48m^{2}ha^{-1} to 48.68m^{2}ha^{-1} over a period of 23 years. However stem abundance and basal area increased for some species. Among animals, censuses conducted 23.5 years apart for monkeys in Kibale indicate that two species, blue monkeys and red-colobus may have experienced significant reductions over the period. Nevertheless, five other species, baboons, black-and-white colobus, chimpanzees, mangabeys, and redtail monkeys had not changed in abundance (Mitani *et al.* 2000). In Budongo, there was no change in primate numbers over a period of 8 years (Plumptre et al. 2001). As we often do not know how populations have changed and the factors underlying those changes, the subject of population regulation remains poorly known in Uganda's forests.

4.3.1. The Role of Predation and Infanticide

Food availability, predation, and disease outbreaks are all potential factors regulating natural populations. However, there is very little quantitative evidence from Ugandan forest parks that links these factors to population regulation. The most direct evidence concerns predation. Chimpanzees exert so much pressure on red colobus populations in Kibale that their population density is negatively correlated with chimp density (Plumptre and Cox, 2005). There is also evidence that monkeys form 80% of crowned eagle prey items at Kibale and crowned eagles depress red colobus populations by 20% (Mitani *et al.* 2001), although these birds are only thought to remove 2% per year of all the primate populations. Evidence suggests that primate group sizes can remain fairly stable as a result of high mortality of infants and juveniles (Chalmers 1968). This mortality rate may be high, in part because of high rates of infanticide in some groups (Struhsaker 1977, Olupot 1999). The only other evidence of the role of predation pressure in regulating wildlife population comes from a study at Kibale which found that dipteran flies predated on hyperoliid frog eggs, taking as much as 60% of the eggs from the egg clutches (Vonesh 2001) thus keeping the population from further growth as a result.

4.3.2. The Role of Climatic Factors

It is known that populations can fluctuate seasonally and from year to year, but exactly how seasonal patterns regulate population sizes is not well known. Most primates for instance have no birth seasons but birth peaks occur which are neither related to rainfall nor to food availability (Struhsaker 1997). Similarly, rodents vary in numbers between months but not seasonally, and the cycles vary more between years than between seasons (Struhsaker, 1997). Among birds, the raptors show no breeding seasonality, but black and white casqued hornbills do, and form flocks and move about the forest in a nomadic manner out of the breeding season (Kalina 1988). Understorey birds also show breeding seasonality with nesting and egg-laying peaks occurring during the wettest months in Kibale (Dranzoa 1995). Other data show that the abundance of leaf litter herpetofauna in Kibale is significantly lower in the dry than in the wet season (Vonesh 2001), but what happens to them during the dry season is not known .Cassidinae beetles appear to undergo seasonal changes in abundance with peak numbers in Kibale occurring during the early dry season after the long rains (Nummelin and Borowiec 1991).

In plants, climatic factors may regulate populations through changes in rainfall amounts, temperature, and levels of irradiation. However, there are few studies that show how plant survivorship and recruitment are affected by variation in climatic factors. The only studies that have investigated the effect of climate on plant populations have studied links between variation in climatic factors and fruiting at Kibale. Climatic regulation at this level may also indirectly regulate animal populations. Climate is thought to affect flowering and fruiting in plants.

Regular annual fruiting peaks at Kanyawara, but not Ngogo were negatively correlated with minimum temperature during the previous dry season; as such a low minimum temperature produced a high abundance of fruiting trees (Chapman et al. 1999). Fruiting peaked at the end of first wet season of the year. Some studies have investigated the effect of El Niño events (events associated with extremes in rainfall and temperature). El Niño events reduced flower, fruit, and young leaf production (Struhsaker 1997). These results have however not been fully supported by longer term data using more El Niño events. Such data have shown no links between El Niño and level of fruiting (C. Chapman pers. comm.).

Longer-term climate patterns, such as El Niño may also have strong influences on animal population size. In Kibale, mice and shrew species increased in numbers reaching unprecedented densities during the 1983 El Niño and for one year afterward (Lwanga 1994). Similar increases in mice were recorded during the El Niño of 1976-77 in Kibale. El Niño events have not been observed to have any effect on primates (Struhsaker 1997).

Among birds, it has been suggested to affect Black-and-White-Casqued hornbills. These birds had their greatest nesting success during and immediately after the 1983 El Niño (Kalina 1988). The 1983 El Niño was observed to increase the numbers of understorey arthropods at Kibale (Struhsaker 1997).

4.3.3. The Role of Food Availability and Quality

The role of food availability and quality (food chemistry including nutritional, pharmacological and other chemical properties) in the regulation and limitation of animal population sizes and distribution remains a virtual black box in forest ecology. Current knowledge of the influence of food availability (productivity, seasonality, quality, and off-take by competitors) and distribution relates to its role in animal socioecology. For example, differences in inter-individual spacing, adult male interactions, mating systems, grooming, social relations of neonates, intergroup relations and diet, time budgets, vertical stratification, ranging, biomass, and density among different primate species in Kibale can be explained in terms of differences in density, dispersion patterns and renewal rates of the divergent classes of food they eat (Struhsaker 1980). The role of food quality is implied by the preference of frugivores for fruit with high metabolizable energy (Conklin and Wrangham 1994, Reynolds 2005), high crude protein (Baranga 1982), high protein to fibre ratio (Oates 1977a), low tannin content (Gartlan *et al.* 1980, Waterman *et al.* 1980, Choo *et al.* 1981) and tendency to eat soil (Reynolds 2005, Pebsworth *et al.* 2006), dry wood (Mahaney *et al.* 1997, Reynolds 2005), and specific water plants (Oates 1978). It is known that the nutritional value of primate foods varies among trees, time periods, and areas (Chapman *et al.* 2003b). It is also suspected that animals ingest certain 'foods' for their pharmacological properties. However, few correlations have been established between food chemistry and animal population densities, or other parameters of population health.

One such study (Rode *et al.* in press) looked at nutritional correlates with redtail monkey population density in Kibale. Redtail density was higher in unlogged than heavily logged forest. Redtails feed on a varied diet of mainly fruit and insects, but also on items like leaves and leaf buds. Fruit is generally known to be high in energy but low in protein, minerals, and highly variable but generally low in lipids (Review by Rode *et al.* in press). It was found that crude protein, lipids, and minerals were higher in diets of unlogged forest groups than in heavily logged sites. Across heavily logged, lightly logged, and unlogged forest sites, absorbable copper and the ratio of copper to caloric intake in redtail diets were correlated with redtail population density. Another study looked at the relationship between black-and-white colobus and protein to fibre ratio of mature leaves. Protein:fibre ratio of mature leaves was positively correlated with monkey biomass, accounting for 87% of biomass variation (Chapman CA *et al.* 2004). A third study (Wasserman and Chapman 2003) related the abundance of black-and-white colobus and red colobus monkeys in Kibale to food energy and protein and fibre contents of mature leaves of 20 most abundant tree species. Average protein to fibre ratio but not energy content was positively correlated with colobine biomass.

Another study Chapman *et al.* (2006b) investigated declines of populations in forest fragments in relation to food availability and parasite infection. The authors found that red colobus populations in eight forest fragments adjacent to Kibale National Park declined on average by 21% over a period of three years. Food trees declined by an average of 29%, and nematode prevalence was high (58% on average) among the fragments. Change in colobus population size was correlated with both with food availability and the number of incidences of parasite infections. To address problems of small populations, it is clear that hunting and protected area loss need to be minimized, and connectivity between protected areas maintained.

Most of what we know about the link between food availability and population change is however based on analyses of population change following logging (section 6). These studies show that the direction of population change is species- and forest-specific and is strongly influenced by logging intensity. Changes in population are thus interpreted in terms of change in environmental conditions and availability of resources (e.g. food, nesting sites, temperature, light intensity, humidity) of which food is often considered the most important. There are few direct attempts to link food availability or food quality to population change. Four studies have attempted to do this in Kibale and Mgahinga, but sometimes with surprising results.

In Kibale, Butynski (1990) showed that blue monkey densities were 10 times higher in Kanyawara than Ngogo, but Ngogo had a higher tree density and basal cover, greater tree species richness and diversity, and more fruit left uneaten than Kanyawara. Between and within species competition for food were both found to be less at Ngogo than Kanyawara. This suggested that other factors, such as predation and disease but not food availability may be regulating population size of blue monkeys there. At Kanyawara however, findings did suggest population density was linked to food production. In a study of redtail monkeys, Rode et al. (in press) found that availability of redtail food was 3.5 times higher in unlogged than heavily logged forest and redtail tail density was more than 3 times higher in unlogged forest sites. Also at Kanyawara, mangabey density increased from 6-7 individuals km^{-2} in 1974 to 13-14 individuals km^{-2} in 1991. This increase was shown to correspond with an increase in mangabey food tree density there (Olupot *et al.* 1994). At Mgahinga, Twinomugisha (in progress) found that in terms of protein and sugar content, golden monkey food did not differ from that of their congeners- the blue monkeys- in lower elevation forests. Golden monkeys obtained their sugar from fruits and protein from bamboo shoots. However, golden monkey diet was less diverse than blue monkey diet, and fruit was scarcer in Mgahinga than Kibale. These findings, as well as the observation that golden monkeys have a lower infant:adult female ratio compared to blue monkeys suggested that food availability may be regulating the size of the golden monkey population at Mgahinga.

4.3.4. Parasites and Disease

Parasites and disease occur naturally in the wild, and only become of serious conservation concern when the populations affected are either too small and likely to be severely reduced in size or when infections are of human origin and will have a major impact. In Ugandan parks, apes have a high risk of being infected by pathogens of human origin because of their close relatedness to humans. Other species such as antelopes and pigs also risk becoming infected by pathogens from livestock.

Mass death of animals due to disease and parasite infection has been observed in savanna, but not forest parks. The only documented outbreaks concern gorillas in Bwindi and Chimpanzees in Kibale. Two outbreaks of scabies have occurred in the gorilla population in Bwindi. In 1996, a scabies outbreak was reported in Bwindi which affected two individuals in the Katendegyere group; one a juvenile, which survived after treatment and an infant, which was not treated and died because of difficulties in capturing it (Stewart 1997, Kalema *et al.* 1998, Kalema *et al.* 2002). In 2003, there was another outbreak in the Nkuringo group. This outbreak affected three gorillas which were all treated (Rwego 2004) and recovered after 3-4 months. Scabies is a highly contagious condition caused by a mite that infests the skin causing lesions and hair loss. In Kibale, a 1998 outbreak of a respiratory disease among the chimpanzee community at Kanyawara killed an adult female chimpanzee (Gladys Kalema, personal communication) and in Budongo, there was a similar outbreak in November 1999 affecting 23 Sonso chimpanzees but the epidemic disappeared without any loss of life (Report by Gladys Kalema in Reynolds 2005).

Circumstantial evidence of population changes in forest fragments suggests that parasites may regulate animal populations in parks. In a study of red colobus populations in forest fragments adjacent Kibale National Park, Gillespie and Chapman (in review) found that red colobus but not black-and-white colobus populations in the fragments declined by 20% over a period of four years. They found that infection prevalence and the magnitude of multiple parasite infections in these fragments were greater for red colobus than black and white colobus. As a result of these observations, several studies have looked for parasites in wild animals. For example, Pebsworth *et al.* (2006) have documented 7 species of helminth and one species of protozoan parasites found in fecal samples of Budongo and Kibale chimpanzees and Rothman *et al.* (2006a) have listed helminth (10 species), cestode (1 species) protozoan (3 species), and arthropod (2 species) parasites found in Bwindi gorillas. Gillespie *et al.* (2005) have listed nine helminth and three protozoan parasites found in the two colobus species in Kibale and *Colobus angolensis* near Lake Nabugabo.

The risk of mortality in wild populations from infections of human origin has been assessed indirectly by identifying potential sources of infection and transmission routes. One such study has shown a high prevalence of diseases common to chimpanzees and humans among communities living adjacent to Kibale National Park (Adams *et al.* 2001). Tourists visiting Kanyanchu tourist facility and villagers living in the adjacent Bigodi community had a high prevalence of diarrhea and infectious diseases, and also had respiratory disease symptoms (Adams *et al.* 2001). Another study in Bwindi (Nizeyi *et al.* 2004) found that the prevalence and intensity of shedding of *Cryptosporidium parvum* oocysts and *Giardia duodenalis* cysts by cattle grazing in the vicinity of the Bwindi was high, and since these parasites recovered from cattle are capable of infecting humans and gorillas, it was concluded that cattle grazing near Bwindi should be considered as a significant reservoir of these parasites. At Budongo, potential parasite transmission between humans and primates has been demonstrated for chimpanzees. Mugisha (2004) found that chimpanzees were infected with helminths of *Strongyloides*, *Strongyles*, hookworms, *Ascaris*, *Trichuris*, *Enterobius*, and *Anoplacephala* species. There was a higher prevalence of *Ascaris* among project employees than other people of the neighboring community. Other parasites found to occur in people were *Strongyloids*, hookworms, *Shistosoma mansoni*, and *Giardia*.

In Bwindi, one study noted that the protozoans of the genus *Cryptosporidium* are capable of infecting humans and gorillas. The protozoans form cysts outside the gut, and when ingested, endogenous stages inhabit epithelial cells of the gastro-intestinal, respiratory, or renal tracts of vertebrates (Sebunya 2000). They were more prevalent among park staff than in the people living near the park boundary, whereas none was found among tourists and UPDF soldiers in the area. Observed risk factors in transmission of the parasite from gorillas to humans included drinking of water from park streams and contact with gorilla dung. Potential risk of transmission from humans to gorillas was considered to be from the disposal of human fecal waste within Bwindi Impenetrable National Park.

Another study based at Bwindi looked at routes of infection of *Capillaria hepatica*, a liver roundworm that causes liver infection (capillariasis) in gorillas. The worm is cosmopolitan, inhabiting a range of hosts including humans, vervet monkeys, chimapanzees, rats, mice, and squirrels. Capillariasis is thought to be common among animals that live at the edge of park, where they interact with humans (Makanga 2002). Infection in rats is so lethal that it is used to control them in Australia. Parasites were detected in two (*Dasymys incomtus* and *Arvicanthus niloticus*) out of 14 rodent species analyzed. The authors recommended that control of capillariasis in gorillas should take into account this transmission route (Makanga *et al.* 2004).

Among non-primate species, links between wildlife diseases and human-related diseases have been investigated for African Swine Fever. African swine fever is an acute to chronic febrile viral disease of the pig family (Suidae). It is characterized by a high fever, hyperemia of the skin and hemorrhages in many internal organs especially the lymph nodes. It is endemic in wild swine such as the warthog, bushpig, and giant forest hog. Wild swine rarely show clinical signs, and only the young animals may shed the virus. Biological transmission from wild to domestic swine is through a soft tick, *Ornithodorus moubata*. In Uganda, the disease has greatly retarded pig farming. Analysis of serum samples from wild pigs (but not giant forest hogs) in Queen Elizabeth National Park tested positive for antibodies to African Swine Fever virus swine (Sepiria 2000). There is potential for spread of African Swine Fever from wild to domestic pigs and vice versa where the areas used by the two overlap. As human pressure increases on national parks, so will be the need to identify potential disease agents and transmission routes to prepare contingency plans for disease outbreaks. Camera traps set in Bwindi have shown that people move through the forest with their pigs when walking to the market. Studies of disease transmission risk among people, wildlife, and domestic animals will increase in importance as a basis for interventions safeguarding animal health, human health, and wildlife conservation in protected areas (Goldberg et al. 2008).

4.3.5. The Role of Isolation and Population Size

All threats to wildlife populations and their biological and physical environments will, if sustained, eventually lead to population declines. However, the extent of isolation and forest size also determine population size. This can be seen from differences between Kibale and Itwara. Itwara is a small forest which is only 15% the size of Kibale. It has five or six anthropoid primate species compared to the eight found in Kibale, even though the two forests are only some 10 km apart. People living around Itwara are not known to hunt primates. Quite possibly, the red colobus monkey, the grey-cheeked mangabey, and l'Hoest's monkeys have become extinct in Itwara as a consequence of small size of forest (Struhsaker 1981a). Declines resulting from forest reduction may however not be immediately apparent as they may be masked in the short term by crowding of animals into remaining forest.

Contrasts between the primate fauna in Kibale and the small (1-2 km^2) relic forest patches on public land a few km to the west of Kibale are even more striking. Surveys conducted in these relics during the 1970s indicate absence of most anthropoids except for the more common redtail monkey and black-and-white colobus. Studies are now only beginning to document what circumstances lead to population decline following isolation and reduction in size of a forest fragment (Chapman *et al*. 2006a, Chapman *et al* 2006b). It is generally accepted that small populations have little capacity to survive in the long term as factors such as disease, genetic variability and demographic stochasticity eventually take their toll. It is also possible that such populations succumb to poaching or to increased conflict with humans as a result of displacement and confinement to small areas. On the other hand, overpopulation of the habitat may lead to population crashes from density-dependent factors such as shortage of food or disease outbreaks. We rarely have the data to tell whether natality or mortality are density-dependent except in a few very extreme cases. Situations close to that have been observed in savanna but not forest parks. In the savannas, build-up of elephant populations in Murchison Falls National Park necessitated culling to save the habitat and elephants (Laws *et al*. 1975).

Chapter 5

PLANT DYNAMICS

Central to park management is a "hands off" policy that maintains parks in their natural states by minimizing human impacts in the parks. This policy is guided by two key ecological perspectives. First is the concept that wildlife populations, species, communities and components of their physical environment are interlinked, and disturbance of one part of the ecosystem inevitably impacts others in ways that are difficult to predict. Since we cannot reliably predict the full ramifications of any human activity, it is best that activities are kept at minimal levels. The second concept is that irreversible changes can occur beyond threshold levels. Human activities need to be controlled to ensure they do not superceed the normal variation occurring in nature. In this section, we review evidence of linkages among species in Uganda's forest parks. This section deals with mechanisms of forest regeneration.

5.1. TREE REGENERATION AND FOREST RESTORATION STUDIES

Managers may be faced with situations in which they have to make decisions concerning the best interventions to facilitate forest recovery following anthropogenic disturbance or to manipulate a forest to increase productivity. Central to decisions on restorative measures is the question: how does the forest recover and what regenerative pathways follow different types of disturbance in different sites? The history of logging in Uganda's forests in the 1930s – 1990s means that most forests have been disturbed. As with other sections, there is limited information in this area. Most of the existing information comes from studies at Kibale National Park and Budongo Forest Reserve.

The process of filling a forest gap, an open edge, or other disturbed site in a forest begins with the arrival of a seed and its germination. Whereas we know that only a proportion of dispersed seeds germinate and a small proportion of seedlings survive to sapling stage, and an even smaller proportion survive to become poles and eventually mature trees, we have no idea for instance how much seed of the same species needs to be dispersed in an area for one tree to survive to maturity. Processes determining tree survival at different growth stages are not clearly known, and the length of time it can take a mature tree canopy to re-form in a given disturbed area is very difficult to predict, yet ideally this is what a protected area manager should be able to manage, particularly where a forest is subjected to extractive management for timber. Observations of regeneration in different forests following different types of disturbance suggest that recovery pathways differ according to the nature, spatial scale, and frequency of disturbance as well as the site disturbed.

Even in the absence of human disturbance, the forest ecosystem, like other ecosystems is a dynamic one where plant density and composition change from time to time influenced by biotic factors such as aging, predation, disease, and competition, and abiotic factors such as rainfall, aspect, slope, and altitude. In one study at Kibale for instance Chapman *et al.* (1997) found significant change in tree regeneration over a period 28 years (between early 1970s and 1992) whereby twenty-seven percent of the focal species increased in abundance, 33% decreased, and the rest remained relatively unchanged. Where the forest regenerates following a disturbance, a typical pathway is that the gap created as a result is covered by fast-growing early succession tree species such as *Albizzia* spp, *Trema orientalis, Maesopsis eminii, Milletia dura, Celtis durandii, Olea welwitschii, Funtumia africana* and *Polyscias fulva* depending on the forest. However, this occurs where the gaps are small. Where logging creates large gaps, recovery of tree cover is more difficult and the gaps are colonized by a dense growth of herbs, climbers, and grasses that choke seedlings. In Bwindi, large gaps are colonized by bracken fern *Pteridium aquilinum,* an understory herb *Mimulopsis solmsii,* and a herbaceous climber *Sericostachys scandens.* In Kibale, such gaps are colonized by the herb *Acanthus pubescens* and elephant grass *Pennisetum purpureum.* Tree seedlings (of *Uvariopsis* and *A. grandibracteata*) that under *Acanthus* are smothered by collapse of a large network of stems during the wet season (Paul *et al.* 2004). In Budongo, *Acanthus* facilitates forest expansion into the surrounding fire-swept grasslands, forest expansion being fastest in areas where an *Acanthus* belt separates the grassland and high forest formations (Eggeling 1947). In logging gaps however, regeneration can be smothered by a variety of climber species, mainly *Momordica foetida, Pyrecantha sylvestris,* and *Solanum* spp. It has been shown that there is a succession of climbers that take over from each other as a gap matures (F. Babweteera, pers. comm.). It has been shown that climber smothering greatly increases in gaps larger than 400 m^2 in Budongo Forest (Babweteera *et al.* 2000) and that managers should aim to keep gaps below this size if they want to encourage faster regeneration.

Recovery of such gaps tends to be complicated by other factors such as fire and elephant browsing that slow down or prevent tree regeneration (Struhsaker *et al.* 1996). Recovery of tree cover at times appears to be slowed at the seedling level as seen from findings at Kibale that showed that seedling density and species richness is as high in logged as in unlogged areas yet sapling density is lower in heavily logged areas (Chapman and Chapman 1997).

As anthropologically degraded forest is still widespread within protected areas, facilitating their reforestation becomes increasingly important. Understanding regeneration is important for devising the best measures to restore tree cover in formerly encroached sites at Mgahinga, Kibale, Mt. Elgon, Semliki, former soft-wood plantations at Kibale and Mt. Elgon and in the heavily logged areas of Bwindi, Kibale, and Budongo. Manipulative restoration of disturbed areas may lead to establishment of different plant communities in rehabilitated sites depending on the type of manipulation. Cuttings planted to serve as dispersal foci or sowing seeds did not speed up regeneration in Kibale (Chapman and Chapman 1997) and weeding may not necessarily promote regeneration of indigenous trees (Chapman *et al.* 2002b). Planting pine trees *Pinus carribea* can promote regeneration of native trees in derelict areas. Kibale pines supported 1.5 times the density and diversity of native woody stems than *Cupressus* and much better than in grasslands left intact (Fimbel and Fimbel 1996) suggesting that forest reestablishment was faster under a "nurse' tree crop, even an exotic species, than if grasslands are left to recover without management. However, a recent study has shown that assisted regeneration may not be necessary in Kibale. Between 1989 and 2003, Kibale grasslands and formerly encroached agricultural sites regenerated to bushland/woodland communities at a rate of more than 1% per year (Laporte et al. 2008). These researchers have argued that natural regeneration in grasslands should infact be halted anthropogenically to sustain persistence of grassland dependent species.

This process of planting a 'nurse' tree crop is commonly used by foresters to encourage slower growing species that are planted under these trees. In Budongo Forest *Maesopsis* is thought to be a potentially good 'nurse' tree because it is a valuable timber species and yet grows quickly and can be used to encourage mahogany saplings to regenerate. Climber cutting around regenerating trees and poisoning of trees considered weeds were also found to be very effective in

Budongo at encouraging mahogany growth and regeneration (Dawkins, 1955). Research in Budongo has shown that climbers in tree crowns can increase tree mortality from 3% to 15% (A. Plumptre unpublished). Although use of a nurse pine crop in Kibale can speed up regeneration rate, one study has shown that enrichment planting in the pine plantations does not speed up regeneration rates (Omeja and Chapman, unpublished data).

5.2. SEED DISPERSAL

Seed dispersal by frugivores is essential for the survival of tree populations as seed survival in fallen fruit does not appear to be sufficient to maintain populations of many tropical tree species. It is thought that seeds that fall to the ground around a fruiting tree suffer high competition from the parent tree and are more prone to being predated by rodents or being killed by disease because of the concentration of seeds around the base of the tree. Many researchers now believe that to maintain certain tropical forest trees, it is critical to maintain frugivore populations. Kibale primates for instance consume fruit and potentially disperse seeds of 87 tree species (Lambert 1998) and 60% of the 25 tree species sampled by Chapman and Chapman (1994a) could potentially be lost if all frugivores were lost from a forest.

Many forest animals of various sizes and taxonomic groupings are seed dispersers, carrying seeds away in their guts from parent plants and depositing them far away which probably increases their probability of germination and survival. Passage of *Balanites wilsoniania* seeds through elephant guts for instance increases their probability of germination by over 50% (Chapman *et al.* 1991) or by as much as 4,000% (Cochrane 2003) in Kibale. In Kibale, major stands of robusta coffee (*Coffea canephora*), found in the eastern section of the central block, are probably maintained by forest animals and birds. The stands occur in areas of relatively open forest and poor tree regeneration. Ripe fruits are taken by redtail and red colobus monkeys, bats, and birds but the epicarp and seeds are discarded (Kasenene 1998). In the Ngogo study area of Kibale, seed dispersal by animals was important for the recovery of burnt sites. Stems of animal-dispersed trees were twice as common in burnt sites within one year of burning than stems of non-animal dispersed trees and were consistently higher within 9 and 25 years after burning. In sites excluded from fire for over 30 years, more than 90% of the stems were of animal dispersed trees (Lwanga 2003).

Detailed studies of the interactions between primates and fruiting trees have illuminated our understanding of the role of dispersers in forest maintenance.

Primates play a role in seed dispersal by 1) dispersing large seeds that are unlikely to be dispersed by a majority of seed dispersing animals, 2) ranging widely hence transporting seeds over long distances from parent plants, 3) improving germination through chemical treatment by gut juices, and 4) improving the survival of seeds by scattering them widely hence making it hard for predators to locate them. Chimpanzees disperse large quantities of seeds. The abundance of large seeds alone has been estimated to amount to 370 seeds $km^{-2}day^{-1}$ Chapman (1995), over 98% of chimpanzee dung samples may contain seeds (Wrangham *et al.*, 1994b) and fig seeds alone may comprise 78% of seeds in chimpanzee dung (Tweheyo and Lye, 2003).

Seeds dispersed through dung which are not found by rodents or secondarily dispersed by dung beetles are probably capable of germination if the conditions are right. For instance, the rate and success of germination of chimpanzee-dispersed seeds has been shown to be higher than seeds that have not passed through the gut (Wrangham *et al.* 1994b). When researchers take seeds from primate dung and attempt to germinate them in controlled settings, evidence typically suggests that the passage through a frugivore improves the rate of germination and reduces latency to germination.

Seed ingestion and its subsequent passage through the gut is one means of dispersal. Seeds can also be dispersed when spat out by fruit eating primates and when those in dung are transported in dung balls by beetles and subsequently buried. Although seed-spitting has been shown to be ineffective at dispersing seeds away from parent trees in Kibale (Dominy and Duncan 2005), processing of the fruits by the animals increases the probability of seed germination. Lambert (2001) observed that processing of *Strychnos mitis* fruits at Kibale by redtails results in a reduction of fungal pathogen attack. Unprocessed seeds were also more likely to be attacked by seed predators. In most fruit-feeding incidences for *Strychnos*, the monkeys removed the pulp and spat out seeds within 10m of the removal site. 83% of the seeds spat out by the redtails germinated, while only 12% of unprocessed seeds survived to germination, while only 5% of unprocessed seeds survived to seedling establishment.

Dispersal of seeds away from the parent plant may not only allow plants to colonize distant parts of the landscape, but also facilitate escape from high seed mortality near parent trees. Dung beetles roll primate dung containing seeds up to 5m from the site of deposition. Burrowing and ball-rolling dung beetles bury seeds at depths ranging from 2.5 to 12cm. The removal and burial of these seeds is thought to be beneficial because the seeds are less likely to be found by rodents (Chapman 1995). By incorporating seeds in the dung, dung beetles could enhance seed survival, seed dispersal and probability of germination. Of seeds placed in dung piles, 69% remained on the surface while 25% were buried. Larger seeds are buried more shallowly than smaller seeds and buried seeds are less likely to be removed by predators than seeds at the surface. Germination of seeds buried at 1- and 3- cm depths is significantly higher than seeds buried at 10 cm (Shepherd and Chapman 1998).

Since the majority of seed dispersers are arboreal, tree-dwelling animals, more seed is dispersed into more wooded than less wooded habitats. For example, Duncan and Chapman (1999) found that seed rain under trees of all heights was greater than in short or tall grasslands in a study of bat and bird dispersal in a deforested agricultural area adjacent to Kibale National Park. Bats dispersed seeds mostly below tall trees, while birds dispersed seeds mostly below tall and mid-sized trees. More seeds and seed species were dispersed under tall trees than below short trees. Nearly all tree and shrub seeds collected were species typically found in disturbed grassland, not in forest. In addition, findings by Chapman and Onderdonk (1998) suggest that forest succession may proceed slowly in degraded lands. These researchers reported that in comparison to the intact forest, forest fragments had lower seedling density and fewer species of seedlings. A greater proportion of seedlings were from small-seeded species that might not require primates for their dispersal, since they probably can be dispersed by small birds. One of the best known avian dispersers are black-and-white casqued hornbills, which mediate long distance dispersal of many forest seeds but for which no quantitative data are available from Ugandan forests beyond lists of fruit ingested (in Budongo, Plumptre *et al.* 1997b; in Kibale, Kalina 1988). Disrupting the complex interactions between dispersers and fruiting trees can potentially have negative and possibly cascading effects on ecosystem processes.

Chapter 6

STUDIES ON MANAGEMENT ISSUES AND PRACTICES

Previous chapters have outlined forest history, their physical and biological environments, aspects of the biology and behavior of key species, and integrated these into an overall picture of the contrasts of the forests and the need to understand them for park management. This chapter describes the challenges to the ideal of preserving these areas in their natural states. Challenges and effects of management actions are described under four main subheadings: 1) challenges that lead to species extinctions and population declines. These include all forms of illegal resource extraction as well as effects of habitat alteration and conversion, exotic species, and political insecurity; 2) challenges related to extractive protected area management practices such as logging and plantation forestry as opposed to that of non-extractive practices such as tourism; 3) challenges relted to human-wildlife conflict; and 4) challenges related to policy in areas such as law enforcement, multiple-use programs, revenue sharing, infrastructure development, on-farm substitution programs, and agricultural development.

6.1. CHALLENGES LEADING TO SPECIES EXTINCTIONS AND POPULATION DECLINES

6.1.2. Agricultural Encroachment and Grazing

Ugandan forests have experienced varying levels of agricultural encroachment and grazing since they were gazetted as forest reserves over seven decades ago. The most outstanding cases of encroachment are those into KNP,

MGNP, and Mt Elgon NP. In Kibale, an influx of agriculturalists into the southern areas of the park began in 1971 when the local administration in Fort Portal allowed settlers to occupy grassland regions to the west of the Park. As these regions became saturated, newly arriving immigrants began to settle in what was then a forest reserve. Without support from central government, the forest department was unable to control the influx effectively. The rate of immigration had increased markedly by 1976, and settlement spread deep into the forest itself as well as into the game corridor. This diminished the effectiveness of the game corridor as a link between the Forest and the National Park and split the elephant population into two isolated subpopulations (Van Orsdol 1986).

Migration into Mgahinga started in 1951 when the forest department degazzeted 10 km^2 to provide people with additional agricultural land (Wild and Mutebi 1996). The Game Department did not demarcate or enforce the Game Act outside the reduced reserve, but under the law the people living in these areas were illegal encroachers. The issue was discussed with the communities during the inquiry that preceded establishment of the park and it was recommended that the park boundary be re-established along the pre-1951 Forest and Game Reserve boundary. The recommendation was implemented in 1991. Land owners ceased cultivation by the end of 1992 and compensation was paid in May 1993.

In Mt. Elgon NP, encroachment started in the late 1960s when persistent raiding by the Karimojong forced the Sabiny people further up the mountain to occupy the areas immediately adjacent to the forest. The population of immigrant people increased in the reserve over the following years alongside an increase in the numbers of the Benet pastoralists who traditionally occupied the northern areas, grazing their cattle in the clearings. This forced the park authorities to excise an area of about 75 km^2 (UWA 2000b).

Between 1950 and today, Semliki National Park was the most encroached of the forest parks with the encroached portion amounting to 73% of the park. Mt Elgon was the next most encroached (34% of the forested portion), Mgahinga Gorilla NP (30%) and Kibale (16% of the forested area) (Howard 1991). Other parks were encroached to a much lesser degree. For example, Olupot (2004) estimated ongoing total agricultural encroachment at the Bwindi boundary at 1 ha. Extent of livestock grazing is less well known, is probably most widespread on Mt Elgon, but likely occurs in most other parks as findings from Bwindi suggest that it can occur even in the best protected parks (Olupot et al. 2009a).

Severe park encroachment usually occurs as a result of breakdown in law and order or times of political instability, but remedies should include use of community-friendly boundary markers (Olupot et al. 2009a). For instance, in the early 1970s, a government drive to increase agricultural production led to the encroachment of Kibale. Local politicians used land to buy political allegiance during the period 1980-83 and encouraged settlement in Mabira Forest Reserve on the account that 'trees don't vote'; and in 1985 the NRA permitted residents of Bundibugyo to cultivate in Semliki forest reserve after they liberated the district in July 1985 (Howard 1991). Protected area encroachment also occurs as a result of population pressure and the resulting demand for land and is therefore particularly acute in densely populated regions such as around Mt Elgon, Bwindi and Mgahinga or as a result of immigration from elsewhere as in Kibale.

Not much is known about the effects of agricultural clearing and grazing in Uganda's forest parks. In Mgahinga, it is clear that it will take considerable time for land that was encroached and cultivated for decades to return to forests. Golden monkeys still avoid these areas today. In Mt Elgon abandoned cultivated areas showed less regeneration than grazed or non-cultivated forest areas, partly because grazing reduced the height of herb and shrub layers, and increased the amount of available phosphates through addition of animal manures (Reed and Clockie 2000). Wherever it is carried out, cultivation generally tends to increase soil pH levels as a result of burning weeds and felled trees/branches. Cultivation significantly increased the levels of soil calcium, magnesium and potassium in the short term as a result of burning (*Ibid.*), but in MGNP, it reduced the levels of organic matter, nitrogen, as well as soil minerals, causing overall reduction of soil fertility relative to areas with intact forest (Lejju *et al.* 2001). At the Mbwa tract of BINP, cultivation tended to impoverish soil texture by making the soil sandier and increased the clay content, with less silt (Mwima and McNeilage 2003). However, the effect of grazing depends on its intensity and results may differ if grazing is more intense. Intensive grazing in Mt Elgon reduced tree species diversity and abundance of understorey tree flora including the abundance of tree seedlings and saplings while low intensity grazing increased the rate of tree regeneration by clearing *Mimulopsis alpina* that smothered ungrazed areas (Reed and Clockie 2000).

Direct evidence of the impact of human activities on natural populations comes from observations of the community of 13 chimpanzees inhabiting Kasokwa forest reserve south of Budongo Forest. The reserve is 73 ha of riverine forest isolated from Budongo by only 2km of cleared, cultivated and settled land (Reynolds *et al.* 2003, Reynolds 2005). Isolation of the reserve has greatly altered the behaviour of the chimpanzees and imperilled their long-term survival. Kasokwa forest was until recently joined to Budongo along the line of River Kasokwa. The forest area is smaller than the area that would be used by a similar number of chimpanzees under less restricting conditions. Like chimpanzees of the Sonso community in Budongo, Kasokwa chimps feed on the forest fruits when available and take other foods commonly utilized by forest chimpanzees, such as leaves, shoots, and flowers. They also feed on honey and make leaf sponges to drink water, and hunt monkeys. Unlike chimps in larger forests which are usually rather noisy, the Kasokwa chimps keep silent most of the time and do not engage in the loud pant hoots and choruses characteristic of chimps. They are elusive, and hard to habituate. Although they subsist mainly on forest foods, when forest food is short, they are forced to raid, mainly mangoes and sugarcane from the neighbouring villages. Because the villagers stone them while on mango trees, it is said that the chimps have resorted to carrying stones in their hands after crop raiding, although it is not known what they use these stones for. Dr. Vernon Reynolds, in his book on Budongo chimpanzees (Reynolds 2005) describes an incident in which two individuals from this community were burnt alive while in a sugar-cane fields. These chimpanzees have also been recorded reusing nests frequently because the availability of nesting trees is limited.

6.1.2. Illegal Resource Extraction

Illegal resource extraction is a threat common to all Uganda's parks. Harvest evidence suggests that non-timber forest products are generally harvested from forest edges (usually within 1km- Howard 1991; Olupot 2004; Olupot et al. 2009a), while no clear spatial pattern applies to bushmeat harvesting locations (McNeilage et al. 1998). In Budongo Forest where communities only live on the southern and eastern edge there does appear to a pattern of poaching that decreases away from habitation beyond 8-10km. Most forests in Uganda are so small though that it is possible for people to access their centres easily.

Poles and a variety of other non-timber forest products are exploited from the parks by communities. No large scale commercial harvesting of building poles from natural forests has been recorded although there may be limited sale of plant products for medicines and weaving. For montane parks (Mt Elgon NP, RNP, MGNP, and BINP) bamboo is collected for building poles, fencing materials, roofing materials, water piping and, on Mt. Elgon, the shoots are also harvested for food. In low altitude areas, palm nuts (SNP) and rattan canes (SNP and Budongo FR) are among the major non-timber forest products collected (Howard 1991). In some parks such as Mt Elgon, much of the charcoal and firewood used by communities surrounding the parks are collected from the park. Other forest products illegally collected include honey, timber, ropes, mushrooms, crop stakes, and salt (UWA 2000b).

Ungulates are the most commonly hunted animals for bushmeat, while others such as baboons, monkeys, and porcupines are usually killed as a measure to reduce crop losses to wildlife. Primates are only hunted in the Ruwenzoris, Semliki and Mt Elgon. Hunting in most parks is carried out using pitfall traps and snares usually set inside the park, however in Bwindi and Mgahinga, most animals are probably killed in the fields (Plumptre *et al.* 2004). In addition to the hunting of buffalos and small antelopes in Mt. Elgon, colobus monkeys are also hunted for their pelts, used in regalia associated with circumcision rites. In most parks, poachers are mainly interested in obtaining meat for their own consumption and for sale to the nearby communities.

Hunting is probably the single most important factor responsible for the decline of animal populations in parks and local extinction of several species (Lamprey et al. 2003). Poaching is directly implicated for the disappearance of certain species from protected areas. Elephants have for example disappeared from Budongo FR and Mt Elgon NP; buffalo, leopard, and giant forest hog from Bwindi; and yellow-backed duiker from MGNP.

Hunters kill or maim target and non-target animals alike. It is not unusual to encounter chimpanzees maimed by traps and snares set for other animals. Deaths occur occasionally when juveniles are unable to tear the noose from its ground pole. Injuries from snares and traps include missing hands, feet or fingers, so that animals are crippled and have to struggle to climb trees and feed themselves. At Kanyawara, in Kibale National Park, snare rates and densities have been studied (Wrangham and Mugume, 2000) and the snaring rate is 3.7% of the population per year (Wrangham 2001). At Budongo, it has been recorded that 33% of non-infant chimpanzees of the Sonso area suffer from snare injuries (Reynolds 2005). Extensive research has been conducted in Ugandan Parks to understand socioeconomic drivers of hunting with a view to determining community-based solutions and additional options for law enforcement programs (Olupot et al. 2008; Olupot in review).

Where active measures are taken to reduce poaching pressure, animal populations achieve high densities. For example, Mount Elgon National Park in Kenya supports large populations of bushbuck, waterbuck, buffalo, and elephant which may be living at close to carrying capacity. The Ugandan portion supports relatively few of these animals, and no elephants even in the less disturbed parts of the reserve (Howard 1991).

One such active measure is programs that remove snares which have been conducted by researchers at Kibale (Wrangham 2000) and Budongo (Reynolds 2005). At Kibale for example, a snare removal program in the late 1990s eliminated a total of 2,290 snares over 34 months. Snare density varied by habitat but was highest in swamp forests where the density was 240 snares per sq. km. (Wrangham 2000). The study estimated that the overall snare density in the 795 km^2 of Kibale Park was at least 15,000 at any one time. The number of snares varied widely, low during the dry season and high during the wet season. The probability of finding individual animals with snares also varied seasonally, with fewer individuals snared during the dry season.

As a result of these programs, in both places snares became harder to find. At Kibale, snares were increasingly being set in thicker vegetation and more difficult locations. Poachers also started to use techniques designed to make it harder for their snares to be located. For example, instead of walking-off an existing trail to set snares, they jumped off it, so that it was harder for the team to see where the poachers have left the trail. Chimpanzee snaring frequency decreased through the duration of the snare removal program and poachers appeared to focus their effort in an area that included much of the village edge habitat and secondary vegetation, which was difficult to patrol.

6.1.3. Studies of Fire in a Forest Environment

Fire in forest not only kills trees, it reduces the number of tree species relative to unburnt sites, changes plant species composition by favoring fire-resistant trees, fast-growing shrubs and herbs (Nangendo *et al.* 2005). It also facilitates the growth of exotic species. Regular burning of a forest site prevents tree regeneration.

Fire outbreaks are not a common feature in forests, but seasonal incidences have been reported in Bwindi, Mgahinga (Kasangaki *et al.* 2001) and Mt Elgon (UWA 2000b). In Kibale, the grasslands are known to have frequently burnt before the reserve was gazetted as a park.

In Kibale, the forest burnt when local people hunted elephant and buffalo among other animals, and to collect wild coffee (Lang Brown and Harrop 1962). At Bwindi and Mgahinga, fires often enter the parks from neighboring fields, or are those left un-extinguished by honey collectors. Incidences of deliberate burning are rare (Kasangaki *et al.* 2001). In Mt Elgon National Park, wildfires occur regularly in the moorlands, grasslands, and the bamboo forest. Fires result from hunters, bamboo collectors and cattle rustlers, and on the very few occasions when they are deliberately started, they are lit by people protesting over issues of conflict with the park authorities (UWA 2000b).

The extent of areas that burn is usually small relative to park size. On Mt Elgon, sizes of burnt areas have not been quantified, but in Bwindi and Mgahinga, burnt areas rarely exceed 1% of the total area of each park per year and are usually much smaller (Kasangaki *et al.* 2001).

Impacts of fires in forest environments has not been sufficiently studied. Observations of the effects of burning have been made at Kibale, where burnt sites attracted grazers such as the bush pig, warthog, bushbuck and buffalo (Wing and Buss 1970). Effects on vegetation varied according to plant species. Leaves of elephant grass were burnt-off leaving the bamboo-like tangle of stems and roots unaffected. *Erythrina abyssinica* survived unscathed being well protected by thick corky bark. *Milletia dura* trees were burnt back in each fire but sprouted again during the rains and the belt of *Acanthus* at the forest edge was not damaged by fire. The forest belt itself did not burn even in the driest weather (Lang Brown and Harrop 1962).

Repeated burning of Kibale grasslands retarded succession to forest. Observations conducted during 1963-1965 and which hold out to this day, indicated in general that forest cover advanced throughout most of Kibale's grasslands although it receded in a few places that were repeatedly burnt and frequently used by elephants (Wing and Buss 1970).

In the Ngogo study area, recently (<1 year) burnt sites had the lowest richness of woody plant species (9 species) compared to sites excluded from fire for longer periods. Species richness rapidly increased within 9 years of burning to five times higher than recently burnt sites but remained stable over the next 15 years. Sites excluded from fire for over 30 years had the highest species richness. Tree species diversity follows similar trends with a large difference between 1 year and 9 year old plots and between 25 and >30 year old plots but not between 9 year and 25 year old burnt sites (Lwanga 2003).

In Bwindi, burning impeded tree regeneration by reducing the density of younger tree classes (poles, saplings and seedlings). Burning also reduced tree species richness and caused an overrepresentation of fire-resistant species such as *Agauria saliscifolia* and *Nuxia congesta*, and the colonizing species such as *Macaranga kilimandscharica*, *Syzigium guineense*, and *Maesa lanceolata*. It created the necessary conditions for a proliferation of ground vegetation, mainly the bracken fern *Pteridium aquilinum* (an exotic species) and *Mimulopsis solmsii* both of which suppress tree regeneration. In higher elevation areas, burnt sites were also colonized by exotic *Cupressus lusitanica* and in lower elevations by *Lantana camara*. Effects on animals were less clear, but duikers tended to avoid burnt sites, while elephants and bush pigs did not show any affinity for, or avoidance of burnt sites (Musinguzi 2004).

6.1.4. Research on Exotic Species

The types and distribution of exotic species in parks have been studied only in Bwindi and to a smaller extent at Mgahinga and Budongo. In a study of the peripheral 1 km zone of Bwindi, Olupot (2004) found that at least 16 species of exotic plants existed in the park. The general pattern of distribution for most species was that densities decreased from the park edge towards the park interior. Lantana (*Lantana camara*) and tea plants (*Camellia sinensis*) appeared to have entered the park from neighboring fields in the northern sector, while *Cupressus lusitanica* spread through seeding from boundary trees in the cooler southeastern part of the park (Olupot et al. 2009a).

In Mgahinga, exotic plants were found within the formerly encroached 10 km^2 land north of the park (Lejju *et al.* 2001) while in Budongo, the paper mulberry *Broussonetia papyrifera* has occupied the grassland in the sawmill area near Sonso, but is not spreading into the high forest (Reynolds 2005).

Even though studies of exotic species are just beginning, we already know that some exotics have potentially serious impacts on indigenous species. In general exotic species have been known to introduce new diseases for which indigenous species have no resistance, or alter degraded habitats. Invasive exotic plants can choke out native flora and provide no habitat value for native fauna. They can form impenetrable thickets or mats, shading out the seedlings of native plants, competing for nutrients and water, or even fundamentally changing the soil to favor their species. Insects, bird, and other animals that have adapted to use relatively few plant species for food, shelter, or nest sites loose these resources when their plants of choice are excluded (Moore 1998). As a result, they cause species extinctions, or declines, and alter natural processes such as fire regimes in the natural or semi-natural environments into which they are introduced (Williamson 1996, Vitousek *et al.* 1997).

In the United States, exotic species have contributed to the decline of 42% of U.S. endangered and threatened species (Schmitz and Simberloff, 1997) and impacts of invasive species are eventually expected to be severe throughout all ecosystems as increasing numbers of non-indigenous species become established in new locations (US Congr. Off. Technol. Assess. 1993). In Uganda, the best-demonstrated impact on native species is based on observations at Mgahinga where regeneration of indigenous trees was poorer in areas covered by exotic trees than in areas that were not (Lejju *et al.* 2001).

6.1.5. Observations of Effects of Insecurity

Wherever there is armed conflict or widespread insecurity, it is common for local people (and even the antagonists) to become more dependent on natural resources. This is evident from wildlife losses during the national upheavals of the 1970s-80s which are all known to have had devastating effects mainly through hunting, but also through habitat degradation. During armed conflict, the environment is especially vulnerable partly because it often falls low on the agenda of the conflicting parties (Shambaugh *et al.* 2001).

All the six Ugandan forest parks have at one time or another been affected by insecurity through armed conflict and cattle rustling. The most clearly documented effect is a loss of tourism revenue when parks were closed. Tourism was rendered impossible at different times in the Rwenzoris and Semliki NP during the 1990s by incursions of the Allied Democratic Forces (ADF) rebels. The situation was particularly bad for Rwenzori NP which closed to tourism between 1997 and 2001 (UWA 2004). BINP and MGNP were affected to varying degrees by the civil war in Rwanda that broke out in 1990 and continued up to the genocide in 1994 and beyond as rebel groups attacked Rwanda from Congo until the late 1990s (Werikhe *et al.* 1997). There was a halt to tourism over that period in MGNP and in addition when refugees camped near the Virunga volcanoes, they utilized resources from within the parks and destroyed infrastructure. Even when refugees left, infiltration of Mgahinga by interahamwe militiamen made law enforcement in the park very difficult (Ocen 2000). In Bwindi, the massacre of 13 tourists and 1 game warden on 2nd March 1999 by suspected interahamwe militiamen resulted in temporary closure of the park to tourism.

On Mt Elgon NP, the impact of insecurity on tourism activities is less clear. However cattle raiding by Karamojong is thought to be a main cause of cattle grazing in the Kapchorwa part of the park as affected communities drive their cattle there to escape the rustlers. Cross-border cattle rustlers from Kenya also use the park as an escape route between Uganda and Kenya. Some fire outbreaks within the park are associated with insecurity (UWA 2000b).

6.2. IMPACTS OF LOGGING AND PLANTATION FORESTRY

This section reviews studies on selective logging and plantation forestry. Supervised logging by the forest department was only conducted in Bwindi, Budongo, Mt Elgon, and Kibale among the forests under consideration here (Howard 1991). Figures available for harvesting after 1950 indicate that Bwindi was the most extensively logged with logging covering 90% of the park, followed by Budongo with 78% affected by logging. Logging on Mt. Elgon covered 34% and in Kibale 17%. In Kibale and Mt Elgon, softwood plantations were set up to supplement the demand for wood from natural forest.

6.2.1. Impacts of Timber Extraction

Effect on Vegetation

Impacts of logging have been studied widely in Uganda's forests. Impacts start with modification of forest structure by gap creation and proliferation of ground vegetation. In addition to modifying forest structure, logging changes plant community composition. Logging tends to eliminate late successional species in favor of the early successional ones; and where management activity involves enrichment planting and canopy opening through removal of non-merchantable species, impoverishment of communities results. Research in the 1950s showed that mahoganies needed light to survive. Tree planting failed and researchers resorted to arboricide treatment to open the canopy and increase light (Dawkins 1955). As a result of logging and arboricide treatment, Budongo for instance now has higher densities of trees producing fleshy fruits and fruit-eating primates in its logged and arboricide-treated forest areas than it does in its unlogged and untreated nature reserves (Plumptre and Reynolds, 1994; Reynolds 2005). In Kibale, tree species richness, density, and diversity are directly related to the intensity of logging with all these estimates increasing from heavily logged to unlogged forest (Skorupa 1986).

Logging also alters successional trajectories. Under normal circumstances, a gap created by tree death or fall is soon covered by young trees in different stages of growth. Instead in logged situations, dense ground vegetation such as *Mimulopsis* and *Brillantaisia* (in Kibale) or *Mimulopsis*, *Pteridium aquilinum*, and *Sericostachys* (in Bwindi) quickly develops in the opened-up areas. This suppresses seedling and sapling growth by smothering (i.e. suppression occurring from competition for light, space, water, nutrients, and allelopathic effects). In Budongo, logging is shortly followed by development of a tangle of climbers in large gaps (larger than 400 m^2). *Momordica foetida* and other ground vegetation is common in such gaps. The resulting bushy undergrowth is too thick and too shady for the seedlings to penetrate. In Kibale, ground vegetation cover provides shelter and food for animals that destroy seeds, seedlings, saplings, and poles (Kasenene 1987; Lwanga 1994). These effects are more pronounced with heavy logging which creates large and frequent gaps that self-propagate through tree deaths occurring when healthy trees are knocked over by neighboring treefalls (Kasenene 1987, Chapman and Chapman 1997). As a result, ground cover is more abundant in heavily logged than lightly logged sites (Skorupa 1986, Kasenene 1987).

Forests regenerate well when single trees are removed in given areas and the gaps formed as a result is less than 400 m^2 and the canopy is not opened by more than 25%. If two or more adjacent trees are removed, and the resulting gap is more than 400 m^2 and canopy more than 25% opened, climber smothering greatly increases and slows the rate of regeneration (Babweteera 1998, Babweteera *et al.* 2000). In Kibale, subsequent forest regeneration is impaired when the forest is felled by removal of 50% canopy cover using mechanized logging. Heavy felling followed by treatment of "weed" trees with arboricides yielded even worse results in Kibale. It removed a high percentage of the original forest and disturbed 40% of the topsoil leading to a very low rate of regeneration subsequently (Struhsaker 1987, Chapman and Chapman 1997). Budongo had a much higher arboricide treatment but this forest recovered faster perhaps because the Forest Department encouraged cutting of climbers during the 1950s and early 1960s (Reynolds 2005).

Budongo Forest was much more heavily logged and treated with arboricide than Kibale and yet Kibale has shown a much slower recovery of the forest than Budongo has. Not all species regenerated well in logged gaps however. Regeneration of mahoganies such as *Khaya anthotheca* has been poorer in gaps left after removal of parent trees (Mwima *et al.* 2001) and is further complicated by the fact that *Khaya* need to attain a dbh of 80 cm to reach maximum seed production (Plumptre 1996). Poor regeneration from parent tree gaps and removal of trees when or before they attain maximum seed production has the potential to reduce regeneration where there is excessive tree removal (figure 13). Budongo has recently lost much of its mature population of mahogany trees as a result of excessive logging and it is not known how long it will take the reserve to recover them. However, the net result of previous logging and arboricide treatment in Budongo was that merchantable species were promoted, figs increased, and *Cynometra* decreased. It also increased the abundance and species richness of climbers (Reynolds 2005) and the density of *Celtis durandii* (Plumptre, 2006). In Kibale however, heavily logged and arboricide treated areas have shown poor recovery of tree stands and although the growth of young trees in heavily logged areas is increased, mortality is high such that relatively fewer trees are recruited to adulthood in these areas than in unlogged forest. Recruitment from seedling to sapling is poorest in heavily logged areas and the rate of tree mortality is higher in heavily logged forest than in lightly logged or unlogged forest, with many deaths occurring when healthy trees were knocked over by neighboring tree falls (Chapman and Chapman 1997, Chapman and Chapman 2004).

Rates of tree regeneration following logging is also determined by factors other than treatments and the nature of secondary vegetation. Browsing by elephants is commonly cited as one of the reasons for poor regeneration in the heavily logged compartments in Kibale. Elephants preferentially graze in secondary vegetation in large gaps in Kibale (Struhsaker 1997). The suppressive effect of elephant action on forest regeneration in Ugandan forest parks has been recognized since the days they were managed under the forest department.

Figure 13. A *Khaya anthotheca* tree in Budongo Forest. Large mahoganies such as this do not fruit until they reach a diameter of 50 cm or larger. As a result natural regeneration of forests requires large 'seed trees' to be left in logging compartments. (A.Plumptre/WCS)

For example, Lang-Brown (1962) observed that elephants and buffaloes both caused significant damage to vegetation at Kibale, but that the elephant was by far more destructive. Elephants trample on seedlings and damage poles and mature trees in large gaps while browsing. In Budongo, counts of 1967 recorded over 900 elephants. Elephants were shot to keep their numbers down and to encourage natural regeneration and 1966-1967 alone, 327 elephants were shot on control (Laws et al. 1975). Elephants have been eliminated from Budongo in recent decades.

Another effect on regeneration by mammals is the action of rodents, which eat seeds and seedlings. In Kibale, several studies have consistently shown that rodents are most numerous in heavily logged than lightly logged and unlogged forest sites (Struhsaker 1997) but the reverse is true in Budongo. The extent of vegetation community change after logging depends on the nature and intensity of treatment and varies between forests. In general, light, but not heavy logging temporarily opens up the canopy, which closes again within a few years.

Effect on Primates

Primates respond to habitat disturbance in many ways, with some populations declining and others increasing. Observations at Kibale generally contrast with those from other logged forests in Uganda that have been studied. In the Kanyawara study area, frugivorous primates are affected more severely than the folivorous ones (Skorupa 1986) and density of nocturnal primates may be lower in logged than unlogged areas (Weisenseel *et al.* 1993). Five out of 7 diurnal species (chimpanzees, mangabeys, redtails, blue monkeys, and red colobus) in Kibale showed post-logging declines in logged areas 14 years after logging and in some areas, these trends have persisted over a period of 28 years (Chapman *et al.* 2000). Chimpanzees are commoner in three unlogged sites (K30, Dura, and Mainaro) than in logged sites (Sebitoli, K14, and K15). In Budongo, a combination of logging, arboricide treatment, and assisted regeneration increased the overall amount of fruit available to frugivores and hence increased overall primate density (Reynolds 2005). Densities of blue monkeys, redtail monkeys and black and white colobus are higher in logged than unlogged forest in Budongo, while chimpanzees and olive baboons are not visibly affected by logging in this forest (Plumptre and Reynolds 1994). Available data from Kalinzu show that chimpanzees use logged forest more heavily than unlogged forest, primarily because of the high abundance of colonizing *Musanga leo-errerae* whose fruits are heavily used by chimpanzees (Hashimoto 1995). Observations in Bwindi show similar results, with heavily logged mosaic habitat dominated by mature trees constituting optimal habitat for L'Hoest's monkeys (Butynski 1984). The heavily logged peripheral zone of Bwindi also has higher numbers of monkeys than the lightly logged or unlogged inner areas (Andrew Plumptre, pers. obs.)

A common pattern to Kibale and Budongo is the effect of logging on black-and-white colobus (guereza). At Kibale, the density of black-and-white colobus increased to a level 5 times higher than that in unlogged forest (Skorupa 1986), Teleen (1994) found a record total of 67 different guereza groups within 400 ha of heavily logged forest in Kibale. Chapman *et al.* (2000) also recorded significant guereza increases in the heavily logged Kibale compartment, over five times greater than in the unlogged area. Similarly in Budongo, the density of black-and-white colobus monkeys is higher in selectively logged forest (44.2 individuals km^{-2}), than mature un-logged forest (27.0 individuals km^{-2}) (Plumptre and Reynolds, 1994) perhaps because guerezas depend mainly on forest edge and middle story trees which were probably little affected by large tree felling.

It is also possible that there is an increase in leaf productivity as the canopy is opened. Most of the trees on which they feed are deciduous and typical of colonizing situations. Although selective felling may indeed increase the density of guereza food trees over a short period of time, a complete removal of large trees over wide areas would certainly be deleterious even to the guereza (Oates 1977a). A 28-year comparison of primate abundance in logged and unlogged areas in Kibale has shown that primate recovery is fast for one species (*Colobus guereza*), slow for two (*Procolobus badius* and *Lophocebus albigena*), and not occuring at all for two species (*Cercopithecus mitis and Cercopithecus ascanius*) (Chapman *et al.* 2003a).

Studies of logging have also shown that logging may affect primate ranging behavior and health in Kibale. Group composition in mangabey groups occupying logged forest was more dynamic than that of groups in unlogged forest. Adult males frequently moved in and out of groups in logged forest and logged forest groups break up into subgroups more often than groups in unlogged forest (Olupot 1999). Redtail monkeys in heavily logged areas may use larger home ranges, travel further and spend more time foraging and less time feeding than conspecifics in unlogged areas (Stickler 2004).

Finally, mangabeys (Olupot 2000) and red colobus monkeys (Gillespie and Chapman 2006) inhabiting logged forest may weigh less and are likely to be more infested with parasites respectively than those occupying unlogged habitat. In Budongo, ranges of redtails, blues, and colobus were smaller in logged forest and number of infants was higher.

Effect on Other Mammalian Taxa

Effects of logging on other mammals is known mostly from studies at Kibale. Most studies have looked at the effect on small mammals but a few observations are available for large and medium-sized mammals. Elephants commonly browse in large gaps associated with heavy felling more often and more heavily than gaps of the lightly logged or un-logged forest (Struhsaker 1997) and are thus positively affected by logging. Effects on other large-bodied mammals shows mixed results. Logging does not appear to have any effect on bush pig density (Nummelin 1990) and the same appears to be true of bushbucks (Struhsaker 1997). For duikers, Numellin (1990) found that selective logging favored duikers but McCoy (1995) showed that duikers are twice as many in unlogged than in logged forest. Blue duikers were more adversely affected by moderate and heavy logging at Kibale than were red duikers, being more abundant in mature forest with a relatively open understorey. In addition to the effect on abundance, logging also altered duiker behavior. Duikers in heavily logged forest altered their activity schedule and were not as active during the day as duikers in un-logged forest. Flight strategies of duikers in logged forest were also altered: those in logged forest were more inclined to hide than those in mature forest, and their flight distances were significantly decreased. Red duikers were more inclined to use trails in open canopy forest while blue duikers were not (McCoy 1995). Logging may make red duikers more vulnerable to hunting.

Like other animals, rodent communities are not affected by logging in the same way in different forests. In Kibale, Kasenene (1984) found that rodent density was significantly higher in logged than un-logged forest and populations were larger in gaps than in the forest under-storey. Lwanga (1994) however found a higher density in unlogged forest, but no difference in species diversity between heavily logged and unlogged forest. These differences are thought to arise from sampling during El Niño and non-El Niño years. In Budongo, rodents are more abundant in un-logged than logged forest and species richness is similar between the two forest types. There is higher seed predation by small rodents (mice and shrews) in unlogged than logged forest before or shortly after germination (Musamali 1996). The converse is true at Kibale where seed and seedling predation are believed to be higher in logged than unlogged forest.

Effect on Birds

The main effect on birds is alteration of the number and types of species supported by the logged habitat. Species preferring mature forest decrease, while those adapted to broad ecological requirements increase (Sekercioglu 2002). Under-storey birds adapted to low light intensity in mature forest are incapable of handling the higher stress induced by higher light intensity, higher temperatures, and reduced humidity in the logged habitats and as such may be found in fewer numbers in logged forest. Other forest dependent species may be reduced in logged habitat because of reduced food availability and lower density of nesting sites. In Kibale for instance, Kalina (1988) found that black-and-white hornbills were present in higher numbers in primary forest than in logged forest. Species that breed in tree crevices and holes are rarer in logged forest (Dranzoa 2001). Some, such as those that feed on litter arthropods may also be food-limited due to drying and hardening of the soil under disturbed conditions and are rarer in logged forest.

Opportunistic species adapted to broad ecological requirements are favored by logging. Logging also appears to favor transient birds (such as vultures, kites, marabous that are usually found in open habitats) and juveniles of forest species, which are more abundant in heavily logged than lightly logged or unlogged forest (Howard 1991). Logged forest is a favorite breeding habitat for edge and gap species in Kibale (Dranzoa 2001). In Budongo, gaps and non-gap forest sites in Budongo showed similarities in number of species between the two sites, although non-gap forest sites had a larger number of individuals (Kahindo 2000).

Observed effects on avian densities and species composition may also be determined by time elapsed since logging. Within one year after logging, bird species diversity in compartment W21 of Budongo decreased but bird abundance increased (Owiunji 2001). Logging favored insectivores and nectarivores but not frugivores. In the longer-term (30 years after logging), logged and chemically treated Budongo compartments had more species than unlogged compartments (Owiunji 2000). Five of the 22 species analyzed (Red-chested Cuckoo, the Yellow-Whiskered Greenbul, Rufous Thrush, Green Hylia Paradise, and the Red-bellied Flycatcher) were statistically more abundant in logged forest while three species (Little Greenbul, Brown-crowned Eremomela, and Chestnut Wattle-eye) were more abundant in unlogged forest (Owiunji 2000) suggesting that in the long term more than 50% of the common species are not affected significantly by logging. Species that fed on fruits, nectar, or insects from bark were favored by logging, whereas those that catch flying insects or glean foliage were not (Plumptre and Owiunji 1998). In addition to the time since logging, avian species may respond to logging intensity and changes in floristic composition, but these were not studied.

Effects on Reptiles and Amphibians

The effect of logging on reptiles and amphibians is virtually unknown. Amphibians particularly are thought to be sensitive to changes in microhabitat.

One study in Budongo found that amphibians had a slightly higher density in unlogged compared to logged forest, but there was no difference in species diversity between the two forest types (Plumptre *et al.* 1997b).

Effect on Arthropods

The effect on arthropods is also poorly studied. From the little known, logging tends to increase arthropod densities. Arthropods are more abundant in areas with dense ground cover than those with sparse cover (Nummelin 1989). Details for individual taxa are available mostly for the sub-family Cassidinae (tortoise beetles), which includes dung beetles. No differences were observed between logged and unlogged forest (Nummelin and Hanski, 1989). In Budongo, selective logging increased the abundance of canopy-dwelling beetles but decreased their species richness when comparing the fauna on the same tree species in logged and unlogged sites (Wagner 2000).

Effect on Aquatic Organisms

When logging removes trees bordering rivers, it causes a dramatic shift in the input of terrestrial nutrients (e.g., from leaves and invertebrates), increases light and water temperature, and changes the chemical composition of the water. Increased light increases standing stocks of algae, which restructures the macro-invertebrate communities. Maintenance of riparian vegetation is important because macro-invertebrate community differs between undisturbed streams, logged streams, and buffered streams. A 100m wide buffer may be effective at ameliorating disturbance due to clear-felling (Chapman and Chapman 2002c).

Risk of sedimentation and siltation is another problem caused by logging. The risk is higher when machinery is used to haul logs and timber rather than the manual options of cutting, pitsawing, and head-loading timber out of the forest. Whereas damage to nearby trees may be as low as 2% when manual methods are used, use of machinery increases this to 26%, increasing run-off. Tree felling can also cause dramatic changes in flood regimes. For example, removal of 40% of the upper storey trees can increase water yield to forest rivers by 55-70% during the rains as it decreases interception of precipitation and increases run-off and sediment load (Chapman and Chapman 2002c).

Studies of logging impacts on aquatic communities in Ugandan forests are as yet confined to Bwindi (Kasangaki *et al.* 2006). The authors found that medium to high levels of logging and agricultural encroachment increased water conductance, decreased water transparency, and decreased macroinvertebrate diversity. Physiologically tolerant taxa, such as leeches and members of the family chironomidae were dominant in waters at highly disturbed sites, whereas ecologically sensitive taxa of families Ephemeroptera, Plecoptera, and Trichoptera were commoner in the cleaner water of less disturbed sites.

Studies elsewhere have also shown that increased sedimentation and higher turbidity can lead to a decline in plankton through a decline in light penetration. Benthic animals sensitive to mud on their integument and gills, or that lose their interstitial habitats to clogging by silt also decline. Forest modification can lead to a shift of invertebrate communities to burrowing forms less available to foraging fishes. Negative effects of logging on fishes include smothering of eggs and entrapment of fry by consolidated sediments, mortality due to clogging of opercular cavities and gill filaments, and reduced feeding and growth, respiratory impairment, reduced tolerance to disease and toxicants, and physiological stress. Where flooding allows fish to find food, refuge and breeding sites, the consequences of deforestation may be severe (Chapman and Chapman 2002c). In general, findings for Budongo are very different from Kibale due to differences in forest structure and composition.

6.2.2. Research on Plantation Forestry

Research has shown that softwood plantations that were established in grassland areas inside natural forests to meet the country's timber needs have had both positive and negative ecological effects. Softwoods can cause die-back of indigenous trees, suppress regeneration in some areas or facilitate it in other areas. In Bwindi and Mgahinga, the exotic plants introduced can spread through the forest on their own (Lejju *et al.* 2001, Olupot 2004) suppressing regeneration of indigenous trees (Lejju *et al.* 2001). In Kibale, they cause die-backs of some indigenous tree species (Struhsaker *et al.* 1989) but also facilitate regeneration of others (Zanne and Chapman 2002).

In Kibale, softwood plantations were implicated in the dieback of *Newtonia buchananii*, *Lovoa swynnertonii*, and *Aningeria altissima* possibly caused by toxins and pathogens from the conifers, and interspecific competition among mycorrhizae (Struhsaker et. al. 1989). Proximity to softwoods did not have any influence on seedling regeneration. To reduce the risk of tree diebacks and to maintain populations of young trees, it was suggested that conifer plantations of Kibale should be harvested, but in a manner that minimized damage to the soil and existing regeneration, thereby replacing exotic trees with indigenous forests. This was not implemented during the felling operations (1992 – date) which flatten existing vegetation causing as much as 100% damage to the regeneration in most sites.

Other findings in Kibale have demonstrated the role that exotic softwoods can play in establishing connectivity and the restoration of degraded forests (Zanne and Chapman 2001, Zanne *et al.* 2001). Seed dispersing animals used the plantations and tree regeneration was better in plantations than in grasslands. This was because the shade the softwoods provided prevented climbers and grasses smothering seedlings that germinated from the seeds and exotic trees did not regenerate. In contrast, Olupot (2004) found that exotic *Cupressus*, *Eucalyptus* may be invasive in at higher altitudes of Bwindi. Similarly, the black wattle (*Acacia mearnsii*) is invasive at Mgahinga (Lejju *et al.* 2001).

As with plants, plantations have both positive and negative effects on animals. Several primate species (chimpanzees, baboons, black-and-white colobus, and red colobus) feed on leaves and bark of Eucalyptus, and in Kibale red colobus also feed on pine needles. Mammals such as bushbucks frequently use Kibale pine plantations (Zanne *et al.* 2001) and logging and planting pines may increase species richness of Cassidinae beetle species which thrive more in pine plantations than in virgin forest (Nummelin and Borowiec 1991). Similarly, logged areas and intact forest had lower diversity, species richness, and density of leaf litter herpetofauna than pine plantations (Vonesh 2001). Softwood plantations nevertheless support fewer species and populations overall. At one point for example, bird species richness in the Kibale plantations was as low as a third that found in heavily logged, lightly logged, and unlogged forests (Sekercioglou 2002).

6.3. EFFECTIVENESS OF CONSERVATION STRATEGIES

The effectiveness of conservation strategies in preventing park degradation and loss have not been quantified, to any great extent. Conservation strategies discussed in this section include: law enforcement, tourism, community resource management, and integrated conservation and development.

6.3.1. Research on the Effectiveness of Protected Area Management

Illegal activities in the parks are documented during biological surveys, animal censuses, research activities, and UWA ranger patrols. Law enforcement effectiveness can be evaluated by monitoring changes in animal population sizes and trends in illegal activities. Research in individual parks has shown that a variety of illegal activities still occur in those parks (e.g. McNeilage *et al.* 1998,

Olupot et al. 2009a). Comparisons of protected areas are possible through available data collected during chimpanzee and other wildlife surveys in the Albertine Rift forests (e.g. Plumptre *et al.* 2003a). These results show that illegal activities continue in all parks, as well as Budongo suggesting that law enforcement and other conservation activities have so far not been 100% effective. Forest parks (other than Mt. Elgon which has no published data) have however been more effective at minimizing all forms of illegal activity than forest reserves. Agricultural encroachment and charcoal burning are as effectively controlled in Budongo as in forest parks, bushmeat hunting and illegal timber harvesting in forest parks is much smaller than that in Budongo (Plumptre *et al.* 2003a) suggesting that law enforcement is more effective in forest parks than forest reserves.

Detailed analyses of the effectiveness of law enforcement programs for each park are rare, but when made have not provided clear links between law enforcement and the degree of park protection. One study (Baker 2004) compared the effectiveness of patrol strategies and found that multiple day patrols were not more effective than single day patrols. The study noted that the introduction of multiple use programs made law enforcement easier because it reduced community hostility towards the park managers, but it was not clear to what extent law enforcement reduced illegal activity. Another study (Laporte et al. 2008) has used remote sensing to monitor vegetation change at Kibale grasslands following its upgrade to National Park status. The study showed rapid change of grassland areas to forest indicating park effectiveness in excluding fires.

6.3.2. Studies of Effectiveness of Conservation and Development Strategies

Programs linking conservation with development are thought to improve attitudes and support of the local communities for parks. For instance, the hostility of communities living around Bwindi and Mgahinga towards a change of status of these areas from forest reserves to national parks is believed to have been reduced by the park's revenue sharing programs, by permissions to harvest non-timber forest products and to keep beehives in the forest, and by the activities aimed at improving community livelihoods under the Mgahinga-Bwindi Impenetrable Forest Conservation Trust (MBIFCT). Until recently, there was little quantitative assessment to verify that it was the case. Namara *et al.* (in progress) have examined six ICD strategies: sustainable agriculture programs and on-farm substitution which aimed to reduce demand for park resources; and multiple use, tourism, revenue sharing and a local conservation trust fund which aimed to provide communities with sustainable benefits derived from the parks.

The study found that community attitudes to the parks have improved greatly since gazettement, and that ICD strategies played an important role in this. The poorest people generally had less positive attitudes, but when they received park-related benefits, it led to a higher level of attitude change than for richer people. Problem animal damage to crops had a negative impact on attitudes, and while this damage seemed to affect different wealth categories equally, the negative impact on attitudes of the poor was much greater. Community cooperation with park authorities has also improved, particularly the willingness to assist in fighting fires and to a lesser extent reporting of illegal activities. The study concluded that ICD strategies have, through their impact on community support for conservation, reduced some of the threats to biodiversity in Mgahinga and Bwindi, in particular fires and politically driven threats (e.g. degazettement, roads). Overall, ICD strategies do not seem to have had major impact in reducing illegal forest resource exploitation (Baker 2004, Namara *et al.* in progress) perhaps because illegal activities are mainly conducted by poorer people and many of the strategies have not had an impact on the lowest wealth categories. ICD strategies have made the protected area authority's work easier, through improved community cooperation, and have the potential to reduce the cost of law enforcement (Hamilton *et al.* 2000, Namara *et al.* in progress).

6.3.3. Studies of the Effectiveness of Community-Based Natural Resource Management

Community-based natural resource management (CBNRM) programs involve local communities in managing forest resources as a way to enlist local community support and reduce the cost of law enforcement. Legal extraction of resources in forest parks under multiple use agreements with neighboring communities started in Bwindi Impenetrable and Mgahinga Gorilla National Parks, under the concept of zoning initiated through a survey conducted by the New York Zoological Society and developed by the CARE DTC Program in 1988. It was introduced as one way to reconcile the needs of the communities with forest conservation. Staff from the Bwindi and the DTC project with residents of three of the civil parishes adjoining the park embarked on a pilot process of planning and evaluating resource use in 1992. As with all processes towards CRM agreements, the process was a lengthy one. At Mgahinga Gorilla National Park, the process began in 1993. Harvesting under these agreements started in Bwindi in late 1994. A system for rapid assessment of the vulnerability of key resources to specialist users around Bwindi was used to identify species that the communities would be allowed to harvest (Wild and Mutebi 1996). In Kibale, CBNRM agreements were developed with assistance of the Kibale and Semliki Conservation and Development Project (KSDP) over two years (Purna *et al.* 2004). Agreements permitting placement of beehives in the designated zones of the parks were reached later with communities around these parks. Using mechanisms to ensure that communities stuck with the recommended quotas, it was hoped that sustainability would be achieved. However, the effectiveness of these methods in ensuring sustainability has rarely been measured.

As a result of these agreements, surrounding communities are now more supportive and protective of the parks (Wild and Mutebi 1996, Purna *et al.* 2004, McNeilage *et al.* in progress). Around Bwindi and Mgahinga, members of the community used to start fires in the parks intentionally to express their resentment, but fire incidences have long since reduced and communities are now willing to participate in putting them out (Kasangaki *et al.* 2001), and the same is true for Kibale. In Kibale, resource users have in some cases arrested poachers, removed snares, confiscated their tools, and handed them over to the park authorities (Purna *et al.* 2004). Also around this park, over 60% of surrounding residents believe that the park had helped their household through revenue sharing and other community conservation programs, while 34%, mainly those close to the park boundary where crop raiding by wild animals is rampant believe that the park has harmed their households (Goldman et al. 2008). These observations are however contrary to findings from a survey of attitudes of the people living around Mt. Elgon, Semliki, Kibale, and Lake Mburo National Parks. This survey found that people with community-based conservation activities in their areas reported 17 times more benefits from the park than people without these programs in their areas (Mugisha *et al.* in prep). Most people reported more interest in the security of their crops than wildlife, and in access to, but not protection of resources. As such, they do not perceive that unlimited access will produce loss of the resource in the long term. However, CBNRM agreements might sometimes be violated intentionally or unintentionally. Three key issues that need to be investigated under multiple use agreements are whether resource users stick to assigned resources, assigned quotas, and to the assigned areas. Two studies have attempted to measure this, one focusing on harvest impact on three Bwindi plants harvested under multiple-use agreements (Bitariho *et al.* 2006, Ndagalasi *et al.* in press), the other on up to 90 Bwindi plants, 42 of which communities are permitted to harvest under the agreements (Olupot et al. 2009b).

Bitariho and colleagues found that harvestable stems of *Loeseneriella apocynoides* (used for basket weaving) was depleted in all multiple use and non-multiple use zones, while *Ocotea usambarensis* and *Rytiginia kigeziensis* (whose barks are used for medicines) were barely harvested in multiple use zones and non-multiple use zones alike. On the basis of these findings, these researchers recommended withdrawal of *Loeseneriella* from multiple-use agreements, but that recommended quotas for *Rytiginia* and *Ocotea* be increased. On the other hand, the assessment of 90 species around the outer 1 km edge of the entire park in multiple-use and non-multiple use zones not only showed similar results for these three species, but that overall, only a few species of the many extracted are severely depleted (Olupot et al. 2009b). The majority of the species studied (90%) were equally abundant on the edge as in the interior and some species were actually more abundant at the forest edge than the interior suggesting that they were not being overharvested. The following species were very rare and required further assessment of status: the palm *Raphia farinifera* (leaf buds are harvested for weaving), the climber *Rynchorsia hirta* (leaves are harvested for medicine), the liana *Rhoicissus tridentate* (leaves harvested for medicine), the herb *Pachycarpus scweinfurthii* commonly found in the park grasslands (tubers are harvested for medicine), the herb *Gladiolus psittacinus* commonly found in burnt areas in the northern part of the park (bulbs are harvested for medicine), and the herb *Marantachloa purpurea* (stems are used for weaving).

Around BINP, there seems to be declining interest in resource exploitation as a means of livelihood as people become involved in local income generating activities run by NGOs around the park, as well as government programs on health, education, and poverty. The provision of health centres at every sub-county, universal primary education, the poverty eradication action plan, and plan for the modernization of agriculture have provided alternatives (Bitariho *et al.* 2006).

6.3.4. Studies of Ecological and Behavioral Impacts of Tourism

Effects of tourism/ecotourism on subject animals and the forest environment have not been studied well, and whatever is documented is based on observations of gorillas at Bwindi. Gorillas become used to people over a period of about six months when visited each day by people, a process called habituation. Studies on the effects of habituation show, however, that habituated gorillas are more likely to range out of the park than un-habituated ones, and each of the tourism groups in Bwindi have several times been observed in the neighboring fields and homesteads where they forage on bananas and secondary vegetation in overgrown fields. Goldsmith (2001) and Goldsmith *et al.* (2006) observed that when habituated, gorillas; 1) incorporate more non-forest foods (e.g. banana pith, Eucalyptus bark), 2) travel shorter distances daily, and 3) nest in a more cohesive fashion and often re-use preferred sleeping areas over consecutive nights. This behavior increased the possibility of conflict, and disease transmission with people. Habituated gorillas also spend more time outside the park than unhabituated ones. Over a half of the Nkuringo group range for example lay outside the park, and while there they came in contact with garbage, old clothes and other fomites used by humans (Rwego 2004).

A more substantive study specifically looked at the effects of tourism on gorilla behavior in three tourist groups at Bwindi i.e., Mubare, Habinyanja, and Nkuringo (Muyambi 2004). Presence of tourists caused gorillas to bunch up, feed less, travel more, and scratch more. Actions like pointing, sudden movements, making noise, or spreading out of tourists startled gorillas and often caused the gorillas to flee, charge, flatten vegetation, or shield their heads when vegetation was cut over their heads. Gorillas were most disturbed when tourists were less than 7 m away. Effects on gorilla behavior did not change much when tourist numbers were slightly increased or decreased. It is not clear whether gorilla responses to tourists will change with time under similar circumstances. In the meantime however, the study recommended enforcement of existing gorilla rules which were not strictly observed, and increased the minimum viewing distance to 7 m from 5 m.

Despite the rules, new data collected at Buhoma between February and December 2004 (Sandbrook and Semple 2006) show that set rules are not observed. The closest distance between tourists and gorillas was 2.76m on average, and there were several incidences of actual contact initiated by by both gorillas and tourists but tourists initiated contacts more often. Contacts initiated by gorillas were however closer but shorter than those initiated by tourists. The results reinforce previous suggestions that the present rules may be failing, and that the risk of disease transmission may be even greater than previously thought.

6.4. HUMAN-WILDLIFE CONFLICT

Most of the conflicts between people and wildlife stem from crop damage caused by wildlife, and to a lesser extent killing of livestock by predators. Incidences of livestock killing by forest animals are rare, though communities may sometimes complain about the killing of sheep and chickens by baboons and chimpanzees (Olupot 2004; Reynolds 2005). The problem of crop damage is exacerbated by cultivation that abuts protected area boundaries. Factors determining the severity and probability of crop raiding have generally not been well studied, and the best possible information is from studies of elephants. Around forest reserves, crop raiding by elephants is thought to peak when crop availability is high; usually during the early dry season. This contrasts with patterns around savanna parks where seasonal fluctuations in forage quality are believed to have a greater influence such that animals tend to crop raid more when forage quality is low (Chiyo *et al.* 2005) such as when the quality of wild grasses declines to below that of crop species (Osborn 2004).

Communities around Bwindi and Mgahinga implicate the following animals as the main problem, listed in the order of importance: baboons and other monkeys, bushpigs, elephants, birds, gorillas, chimpanzees, buffalo, and porcupines (Plumptre *et al.* 2004). Carnivores such as the side-striped Jackal (*Canis adustus* Sundevall) and the African Civet (*Viverra civetta* Schreber) also raid crops in gardens around Bwindi (Andama 2000) and gorillas in Bwindi also frequently come out of Bwindi to raid banana plantations and forage in pastures or banana plantations (Rwego 2004). Crop raiding by elephants occurs in Bwindi but is not common.

In Kibale, up to 17 wildlife species have been recorded damaging crops around the park. Primates may account for as much as 71% of damage events and 48% of the crop area crop damaged (Naughton-Treves *et al.* 1998). Redtail monkeys are the most frequent raiders, while baboons damage the greatest area of crops. Chimpanzees rank lower among primate raiders, and cause less than one third of the crop damage caused by baboons, and one-half the damage of redtails. Black-and-white colobus, vervet, and l'Hoest's monkeys also occasionally crop raid, while mangabeys and blue monkeys are not known to do so. Redtail monkeys, olive baboons, and chimpanzees select different crops or plant parts.

Baboons take roots and other tuber crops ignored by other primates, and feed on the greatest variety of crops. All crop raiding primates prefer maize and/or bananas. Redtails eat only banana fruit, baboons eat banana fruit more frequently than pith, and chimpanzees raid fruit and pith in equal proportions. As with elephants, peaks in banana consumption are associated with forest fruit shortages. Crop raiding is highest when Kibale is short of *Mimusops bagshawei* fruit. Maize raiding is unaffected by forest fruit abundance (Naughton-Treves *et al.* 1998). The overall pattern of crop damage by wildlife in Kibale is such that fields lying within 500 m of the forest boundary lose 4-7% of their crops per season on average and maize and cassava fields are on occasion completely destroyed (Naughton-Treves 1997). The degree to which crop raiding influences attitudes of communities towards wildlife around parks is thought to be high, but its magnitude in comparison to other causes of public resentment like limits of access to resources, limits on freedom of movement through the parks, and the belief that park land is free land that has been denied to the community is not known. In Kibale, although most of the crop damage by wildlife is restricted to a narrow band of farmers living near the forest edge, risk perception among these farmers has been amplified by legal prohibitions on killing wild animals (Naughton-Treves 1997).

At Budongo, primates are also considered to be the main crop raiders, with baboons ranked highest in this respect (Hill 1997, Tweheyo *et al.* 2005). Bush pigs were ranked closely behind baboons while vervet monkeys, weaver birds and doves, and porcupines were ranked third, fourth and fifth respectively. Chimpanzees ranked very low as pests. The five most damaged crops were maize, beans, cassava, sweet potatoes, and finger millet. Farms within 100m of the edge were most raided, while those more than 300m away were mostly not. Local people used snares, traps, ringing bells, fires, stones, chasing, and several other methods to protect crops (Hill 1997). Other parks have not attracted as many studies in human-wildlife conflict. However, in Mt Elgon where wildlife has been seriously depleted by hunting, crop damage by wild animals is not a major problem, although some cases of crop raiding may involve bushpigs and baboons (UWA 2000b).

In general, attitudes of people towards wildlife vary depending on the species. People show the highest hostility to species that cause the highest crop damage (Purna *et al.* 2004, Reynolds 2005). Incessant crop and livestock raiding by baboons and other problem animals have caused communities east of the northern sector at Bwindi to relocate away from the park boundary (Olupot et al. 2009b). Around Bwindi and Mgahinga, gorillas are perceived positively despite negative encounters with man. Even chimpanzees are positively perceived in general, whether at Kibale or Budongo. Around Budongo however, the spread of sugar cane planting is changing the attitude from a positive to a negative one because the chimpanzees are crop raiding more frequently than they used to. By contrast, the attitude is far worse for baboons, and to a lesser extent, bush pigs (Reynolds, 2005). The overall effect of conflict with wildlife is a general resentment of the parks by communities living in their immediate environs.

A serious cause of resentment towards wildlife around parks is the perceived risk of injury or killing of people by wild animals. Such incidences are rare, but nevertheless occur often enough to raise concern. Several incidences have been reported on encounters between chimps and people around Kasokwa forest reserve. One example is an incident in which the Kasokwa chimps attacked a boy aged 6 years in 1998, injuring his genitals. Another incident happened in July 2000, when one of the chimpanzees seized and carried an 8-week old baby up into a tree in the forest. They bit and subsequently dropped the baby which eventually died on the way to hospital. Yet another occurred in 2002 involving two girls each aged 8 years. They were attacked and injured by chimpanzees on the faces, limbs, arms and genitals (Reynolds 2005). In the villages surrounding Kibale, eight attacks by chimps on human infants have been documented. Victims were aged 6-60 months. Chimpanzees attack infants that are alone or accompanied only by women and children. In three cases, children were eviscerated. Injuries to others included loss of an arm or of hands or feet (Wrangham et al. 2001). Around Bwindi, gorillas come into contact with humans only when humans enter the forest. However, there was an incident in May 1997 when a lone silverback left the forest and moved into the vicinity of a village near the park boundary. It ended up biting one person in the shoulder, a wound that required hospitalization, and also dislocating the elbow of a young girl (Stewart 1997).

There has been a lot of experimentation on ways to control human-wildlife conflict (Hill et al. 2002, Purna et al. 2004, Reynolds 2005). Some work has focussed on physical barriers set along the boundaries while others have looked at psychological techniques. Other efforts have looked at eliminating individual problem animals.

Physical barriers include a buffallo wall (a line of stones approximately 1.5 m high and 1.5m thick [Edward Andama, pers. comm.]), which has been set up at the edge of Mgahinga; trenches (1.5m deep and 2m wide), barbed wire, and sharp sticks and stones set up around parts of Kibale; and the living fence of the Mauritius thorn, *Caesalpinia decapitala,* which has been tried in parts of Kibale, Semliki, and Bwindi. Psychological techniques include scare-shooting usually for elephants, pepper spray for elephants, and live traps (wooden structures constructed out of poles and wire mesh large enough to accommodate up to 1 or 2 chimpanzees) for a wide range of animals including baboons and chimpanzees.

Multiple methods may be necessary to keep most of the animals away from any given area. Barriers have proven to be more effective than the psychological deterrents, although the sharp objects' approach was ineffective because the stones sank into the ground and sharp sticks decayed. The buffalo wall has been effective in preventing buffaloes from getting out (Hill et al. 2002); the elephant trenches have been effective against the elephants and bushpigs; and the Mauritius thorn has been effective against baboons and bushpigs in Kibale and Bwindi. Use of live traps in Budongo has had high trapping success for a short time (Reynolds 2005). On the other hand scare-shooting is effective in the short-but not long-term and experimenting with pepper spray was impractical (Purna et al. 2004). In

Ruteete subcounty near Kibale, killing of individual chimps suspected to attack children has not eliminated the problem of killer chimps as the identity of the killers is not known. Other problems with these methods include the high cost setting them up and maintaining them. Animals may also habituate to gunshots, learn to avoid traps, and there is always the risk that the plants grown for the living fence may spread, and become invasive where they are introduced. It also may be very difficult to reliably identify, and then to track down and extract individual problem animals.

Chapter 7

EXAMPLES OF HOW RESEARCH HAS SUPPORTED FOREST CONSERVATION

We here provide some examples of where we see that research undertaken in the forests of Uganda have led to specific management interventions that support the conservation of these forests. This is not supposed to be an exhaustive list but aims to show the variety of interventions that have occurred.

- Studies of forest regeneration have shown that the timber species of highest commercial value often regenerated under bright light. Forest management therefore promoted arboricide treatment to remove the 'undesirable' species and open up the canopy to allow in more light. This management strategy replaced enrichment planting which was shown not to be very successful and was costly.
- More recent research (Plumptre, 1995) showed that many timber species don't produce fruit before they are around 50cm diameter or higher. As a result many were being felled before they could fruit. Management of concessions now demands that two seed trees are left in each hectare of forest.
- Research on the ecology of gorillas and chimpanzees has led to recommendations for the establishment of ape tourism sites in several forests in Uganda, particularly in Bwindi Impenetrable National Park (gorillas) and Kibale National Park, Kalinzu Forest Reserve, Kyambura Wildlife Reserve and Budongo Forest Reserve (Chimpanzees) (Mapesa 2008, Mugisha 2008, Olupot and Plumptre 2008). These include rules about the number of people at any one time with the apes, the minimum distance tourists can approach and also how long they can stay. Much of

the information from these studies was also used to develop Uganda's Great Ape Survival Plan which is in the process of being implemented.

- Surveys of biodiversity in these forests led to the creation of six forest parks from forest reserves in the early 1990s because the research showed how globally diverse these forests were. Further survey data were used to zone the forests for conservation, for local use of non-timber forest products and for timber harvesting as part of the Forest Department's Nature Conservation Master Plan. Biodiversity surveys have also highlighted the forest's global importance. As a result many of the forests have been designated as part of the Eastern Afromontane Biodiversity Hotspot, an endemic bird area and part of the Albertine Rift Ecoregion (the ecoregion with most vertebrate species in Africa – Plumptre et al., 2007).

- Data from the long term chimpanzee and gorilla studies are being used to compare populations across the continent. Lessons from great ape tourism and research studies assessing the impacts of tourists are being used to suggest modifications to the visitation rules and to try and ensure rules are adhered to. Studies of disease transmission to primates in Kibale will also be used to make better recommendations about how to reduce the risk in the near future (Goldberg et al. 2008). Understanding the ecology and behavior of great apes increases our appreciation of their similarity to humans, and there has been a move to try and create a new designation for great apes as World Heritage Species within UNESCO (R. Wrangham, personal communication, 2005).

- Crop raiding studies have resulted in a vermin control program at BFR, which encourages communal guarding through the formation of village vermin control committees (Babweteera et al. 2008). Studies have also resulted in the promotion of cultivation of crops such as chillies that are unpalatable to crop raiding animals around BFR and National Parks (Babweteera et al. 2008; Mapesa 2008).

- Research on snaring incidences and snare densities at Kibale and Budongo have led to snare removal projects in the study sites (Babweteera et al. 2008, Wrangham 2008).

- Research on disease outbreaks and possible transmission between Apes and humans led to the formation of Conservation Through Public Health (CTPH), a national NGO working around Bwindi to reduce the possibility of disease transmission between humans and apes.

- Research has supported the development of action plans for individual species, for example chimpanzees and gorillas based on their conservation status (Mapesa 2008).
- Research on vegetation, wildlife distributions, socioeconomics, wildlife health, human-wildlife conflict, resource exploitation, population surveys and reproduction has supported development of UWA's management plans aimed at reducing threats (Mapesa 2008) and zoning of the parks.
- Research results have provided a basis for evaluating conservation success. For example, research has shown that through the late 1970s and early 1980s when there was breakdown of law and order in Uganda, Kibale retained a larger population of elephants than any other forest reserve in Uganda due to a relatively higher degree of law enforcement. Also, there are higher indices of duiker (blue, *Cephalophus monticola* and red, *C. harveyi*) abundance in the research sites of Kibale than any other forest in western Uganda due to the presence of researchers (Struhsaker 2008).
- There are documented spin-offs not directly related to research objectives. For example, researchers of primate behavior and forest ecology have supported law enforcement activities in Kibale and lobbied for increased protection (Struhsaker 2008) which eventually saw the forest becoming a park. The sheer presence of researchers discourages poaching and other illegal activities in the park and researchers have supported local communities by providing employment, running education outreach activities, and supporting community projects (Kasenene and Ross 2008).

Chapter 8

MANAGEMENT LESSONS

The above summary shows that research has supported wildlife conservation in the parks although there are not many examples. Some research topics such as human-wildlife conflict, resource exploitation, and extent of habitat disturbance usually have immediate applications. Others, such as projects on ecology and behavior have few immediate applications but may be useful later. For others such as restoration of Kibale grasslands, it may take multiple projects and experimental manipulation for applications to be meaningful. Nevertheless, by understanding individual species and their habitat requirements; outcomes of interspecific interactions; impacts of agents of habitat and population change such as fire, disease, and poaching; managers can see what information is needed to support management efforts. Even basic studies of the biology and behavior of individual species should help the manager in several ways, for example by helping to understand the impacts of subtle practices, such as resource offtake of medicinal plants. Results are also used by managers for better management of tourism programs to improve the quality of experience to the tourist while ensuring minimal impact on wildlife. There are therefore several lessons that can be drawn from research and monitoring programs in terms of prescribing management action. These are described below.

1. Organized forest management in Uganda dates back over 100 years, but the protected areas were not demarcated until 30 years after the forestry department was formed. Over the period of their existence, protected forests have at different times been settled, cultivated, and subjected to extractive practices such as timber extraction, extraction of non-timber forest products, plantation forestry, enrichment planting and arboricide treatment. These practices determine to a large extent the nature of tree

cover and the plant and animal distribution we see in these forests today, as do natural factors such as rainfall, elevation, soil type and structure, and hydrology.

2. Protected forests have the highest concentration of biodiversity in the country. The contribution of forest parks to this biodiversity is large, given that they form approximately 50% of protected forest in Uganda. The full range of biodiversity in these forests is however not known, as is the full range of factors and processes governing variation of the populations it contains. In Uganda's medium to low altitude rainforests, species diversity depends on proximity to upper Pleistocene forest refugia of eastern DRC and the size of the forest, with forests in the west being generally more species-rich.

3. Despite active protective measures which have improved for forests which are now national parks, these protected areas continue to face increased pressure from local communities for use as sources of bushmeat, timber, a variety of non-timber forest products and agricultural land. A combination of ranger patrols and community-based conservation approaches have helped reduce this pressure to varying levels of success in different parks. It is however unclear how these approaches will be effective in the long-term, especially if there is another breakdown of law and order or when politicians seek to use protected areas to buy political patronage. Planning for sustainable effective management approaches that can survive the tests of time is an ever present challenge for the protected area manager.

4. Understanding the basic biology and ecological interactions of key species is useful in predicting how given disturbances or management interventions can impact wildlife populations. For example, we know that several tree species germinate better from seeds when they pass through the gut of a primate or elephant and that these species may be essential for the tree's survival.

5. Many plant species are dependent on animals for dispersal and pollination. Forest animals are integral components of ecosystem processes such as predator-prey relationships that keep pest populations in check, others are crucial in decomposers-nutrient cycles that maintain forest productivity. To conserve biological diversity in forests, it is important that natural cycles are maintained.

6. Logging affects different species and forests differently. Effects of logging are complex. Different species respond to logging in different ways within and between forests and we cannot readily apply lessons

from one forest to another without specific studies in each forest. Effects depend on logging intensity and forest composition (both faunal and floral). In Budongo and Kalinzu, logging has both positive and negative effects on species richness, population size and regeneration rate, but these forests have no elephants. Kibale has elephants and a different tree composition and logging can cause: a) a decline in primate densities, b) an increase in the frequency of windthrows, c) an increase in densities of rodents and insects which predate on seeds and seedlings, d) an increase in vegetative ground cover which decreases forest regeneration. Harvesting should minimize both incidental and direct damage to forest and promote forest regeneration. Directional felling and harvesting with wheeled skidders rather than tracked tractors reduced damage to the forest floor. Pitsawing does not damage the forest floor but is inefficient in utlising trees to give an optimum production of sawnwood, In places where logging of natural forest is undertaken, care should be taken to license a few, but not many, people and to mark out and leave trees that provide seed for natural regeneration, and train pitsawyers and sawmillers in less damaging utilization methods

7. For forests that are still actively managed as extractive reserves, it is important to control species that prevent or slow down forest regeneration, or to maintain harvest regimes at levels where critical gap sizes are not reached (around 400 m^2). Some forests can be regenerated more quickly by weed removal in gaps (e.g. climbers) but it should be realized that vines can also be important compositional and structural components for wildlife in forests.

8. Plantations may be used to restore degraded forest lands on four conditions: 1) that the plantations are near or within protected area boundaries, this being because the seed dispersing animals and birds can easily reach there (Chapman and Chapman 1996); 2) plantation trees are not logged early as damage from logging operations may affect longer term regeneration patterns (Chapman and Chapman 1996); 3) potential die-backs from toxins in the plantations are unlikely (Struhsaker *et al.* 1989); and 4) plantation trees are not invasive (Olupot 2004; Lejju *et al.* 2001). Forest regeneration should be assisted only when there is convincing evidence that natural regeneration cannot work. Even then, careful consideration needs to be given for the survival of grassland dependent species (Laporte et al. 2008).

9. Different species are implicated in the failure of gaps to regenerate in different forest forests –climbers in Budongo; bracken fern, *Mimulopsis*,

and *Sericostachys scandens* in Bwindi, and *Acathus pubescens* and *Pennisetum purpureum* in Kibale. Control of these species may enhance regeneration of native trees. *A. pubescens* for example smothers tree seedlings in Kibale. It has been shown that clearing areas of *A. pubescens* and planting appropriate seedlings can be an effective restoration strategy. Harvesting *A. pubescens* may be a viable multiple use management option because it is a common fuel source for cooking stoves in the region.

10. Use of fire in forest management has never been an option, except in early burning of savanna reserves to reduce fire intensity and increase woody growth, or in unlikely situations where it may be used to fight fires set illegally. Each forest park and reserve should have a fire management plan.

11. Community support is especially critical for continued existence of protected areas, as resources available to park managers are limited and political instability always a possibility (Hamilton *et al.* 2000). Integrated Conservation and Development programs (ICDs) have helped to improve community attitudes and support for parks, but a lot more needs to be done to improve people's behavior. Although resource harvesting is not always confined to zones gazetted for multiple use, the majority of plants extracted in Bwindi for medicinal, and other purposes are not seriously affected by resource extraction and monitoring efforts should focus on the few that are. Determining these, however, requires assessment on the ground. Highly desirable species excluded from multiple-use agreements should be monitored in both multiple-use and non-multiple use zones. ICDs should aim to target the poorest people effectively as these are the most likely to undertake illegal activities because they have no other options.

12. Conserving for biodiversity conservation as opposed to conserving for consumptive use is a viable strategy for forest management provided forest products needed for human consumption are obtainable in adequate quantities from other sources. Revenues being generated from some of the forests from tourism are high, particularly where there is ape tourism.

13. Most of what we know from these forests is primarily based on research in Kibale, Budongo, and Bwindi. Few studies have been made elsewhere. There is an urgent need for more studies, to understand regeneration rates and possible forest trajectories, and factors determining them in other forests, particularly Mt. Elgon, Rwenzori and Semliki.

14. Methods to control human-wildlife conflict are not always effective. Several work in the short, but not the long-run. Multiple approaches (such as the use of trenches lined with Mauritius thorn on the outer side) should be applied in the same area at the same time. Planting buffer crops outside of the parks (e.g., tea, coffee) that are not eaten by wild animals in gardens adjacent to parks may reinforce the effectiveness of barriers set along the boundaries. Some of the control methods have the added advantage of preventing livestock, and possibly fire from entering the parks.

15. It may be tempting to ascribe ecological and managerial problems to misinformation or lack of scientific information. Scientific information is often available for sustainable forest management, but this information may be unavailable because it is buried in obscure literature. This book has aimed to synthesise a lot of the available findings of the research in Uganda's forests in order to support better management of the forests in future.

Chapter 9

FUTURE RESEARCH AND MONITORING

Potential areas for future research and monitoring include:

- More research to learn about forest species and ecological processes. Applied research in this area should address the fundamental issue of how tropical forests can best be used on a sustainable basis and how disturbed forests can best be restored to natural states. Most research findings are impractical to apply for protected area management as many are not expressedly designed to answer management questions. A large number for example test ecological concepts, known theory, or contribute to ongoing theoretical debates and are primarily directed to audiences in Universities and the wider scientific community than to local protected area management.
- Research on methods of reducing human-wildlife conflict around forest reserves, focusing on species that cause the most damage, and trialling and testing intervention strategies.
- More surveys to understand population sizes, trends, ecology and distribution of rare and endemic plant and animal species. For example, De Brazza monkeys are only found in Mt Elgon and Semliki and the Mona monkey only in Semliki, but we have no idea of the status of their populations. Similar studies are needed for problem species such as baboons, and those severely hunted such as duikers, bushpigs and giant forest hogs.
- More restoration research, especially in forests such as Mgahinga, Bwindi, and Kibale where severe human disturbance in the past opened up large gaps that are failing to regenerate.

- More research to understand harvest impacts on medicinal and weaving plants of high demand. Possibilities for ex-situ propagation should be explored.
- More research on the biodiversity of forest aquatic systems and their importance globally.
- Comparative and experimental studies on the effects of habitat disturbance should be conducted in the less-studied forests to compare with the better-studied ones. Limited experimental manipulation of the habitat may be needed where researchers are testing critical management questions.
- Research on types and distribution of exotic/invasive plants and methods to remove them.
- More nutritional studies to understand herbivore distributions in forests. Such studies would help understand habitat suitability, for example whether gorilla use of the southern but not northern sector in Bwindi is related to resource productivity, seasonality, and/or quality as opposed to say, temperature or use by people. Baseline data on nutritional chemistry of herbivore and frugivore food are available for Bwindi, Mgahinga, Kibale, and Budongo.
- Monitoring of large mammal populations, particularly elephants, primates, and antelopes every 5-10 years. This should focus on understanding population trends and distribution and poaching pressure.
- Monitoring of ape health status focussing on unusual mortalities and clear signs of probable illness such as long and frequent resting, coughing, sneezing and diarrhoea. The focus should be primarily on those groups visited by tourists but general monitoring of wild groups/communities is needed also.
- Research to support management should adjust to changing times. The strategy for management of forests that are now national parks has moved away from timber exploitation to low impact use and such forests are have fewer incidences each year of illegal activities than in the past. As such, it is important to understand what will happen to these forests under the current management policy. It is important to put more effort into understanding ways of forest restoration following degradation by logging or other prescribed and unprescribed disturbances. It is also important to understand the impacts of the current low intensity use practises, and to understand the impacts of low intensity disturbance on forest species that thrive in disturbed forest conditions. In the long term, it might be necessary to manipulate the habitat to maintain such species.

Long term monitoring is necessary to keep track of such species in undisturbed forest. Such monitoring for each park should include climate data to determine how they are being affected by climate change. Meterological stations should be set up in each park for this purpose.

Chapter 10

SUMMARY AND CONCLUSIONS

Research has been built around permanent research facilities with most information coming from parks with research stations. Early research in the forests was much more applied and aimed at answering management questions. Most of the research in forests has been species-based in the recent decades; looking at the ecology and behavior of individual species. Other major research in forests has focused on the effects of logging and human-wildlife conflict. Research, both basic and applied has contributed to management of forests in many ways, but it is difficult to draw links between specific conservation outcomes and individual projects as many projects have not been expressly designed to generate results that directly support park management.

Whereas long term applied research in Uganda's forests would ideally be undertaken by the line agencies- UWA and NFA, the lack of resources for research within them precludes their ability to undertake such projects, although they have been undertaking monitoring of large mammal species and sample plots on concessions respectively. We believe that if long term applied research is to be revived in Uganda it should be taken on as the role of these research stations who have a long term presence and can plan for longer term research studies. The Directors and individual researchers of each station should work closely with UWA and NFA to plan research that helps managers answer some of the key management questions that still exist. These include topics such as what drives illegal resource exploitation in the parks and reserves, what incentives can be created to reduce illegal activities in the parks, and what methods are most effective at deterring crop raiding by various species. If the research stations took on these research topics, many of which have been identified in UWA's Research and Monitoring Plan, then the relationship between the research stations and the management institutions will become much closer and the research results would be more likely to be used by the managers as a result. In turn, managers should document research results they have applied and how they have applied it, and communicate this information to researchers. This review has illustrated research themes that can directly support conservation efforts and provided examples of the central role that research can play in wildlife management. Syntheses like this can support conservation by helping guide researchers to develop projects that can support conservation directly and helping managers and policy makers better appreciate the central role that research plays in conservation.

REFERENCES

Adams, H. R., Sleeman, J. M., Rwego, I., and New. J. C. (2001). Self-reported medical history survey of humans as a measure of health risk to the chimpanzees (*Pan troglodytes schweinfurthii*) of Kibale National Park, Uganda. *Oryx, 35*, 308-312.

Ambrose, L. (2006). A survey of prosimians in the National Parks and forest reserves of Uganda. In N. E. Newton-Fisher, H. Notman, J. D. Paterson, and V. Reynolds (Eds.) *Primates of Western Uganda* (Pp. 329-343).

Andama, E. (2000). The status and distribution of carnivores in Bwindi Impenetrable National Park, southwestern Uganda. *MSc. Thesis.* Kampala: Makerere University.

Archabald, K., and Naughton-Treves, L. J. (2001). Tourism revenue-sharing around national parks in Western Uganda: early efforts to identify and reward local communities. *Environmental Conservation, 28,* 135-149.

Babaasa, D. (1994). Status, Distribution, and Feeding Ecology of Elephants in Bwindi Impenetrable National Park, Southwestern Uganda. *MSc. Thesis.* Kampala: Makerere University.

Babaasa, D. (2000). Habitat selection by elephants in Bwindi Impenetrable National Park, southwestern Uganda. *African Journal of Ecology, 38,* 116-122.

Babaasa, D., Eilu, G., Kasangaki, A., Bitariho, R., and McNeilage, A. (2001). Gap characteristics and regeneration in Bwindi Impenetrable National Park, Uganda. *African Journal of ecology, 42,* 217-224.

Babweteera, F., Reynolds, V., and Zuberbuhler, K. (2008). Conservation and research in the Budongo Forest Reserve, Masindi district, Western Uganda. In R. Wrangham, and E. Ross, (Eds.). *Science and Conservation in African Forests* (Pp. 145-157). Cambridge: Cambridge University Press.

Baker, J. (2004). Evaluating conservation policy: Integrated Conservation and Development in Bwindi Impenetrable National Park, Uganda. *Ph.D. Thesis*. Cantebury: Durell Institute of Conservation and Ecology, University of Kent, Cantebury.

Baranga, D. (1982). Nutrient composition and food preferences of colobus monkeys in Kibale Forest, Uganda. *African Journal of Ecology, 20,* 113-121.

Babweteera, F. (1998). Influence of gap-size and age on the diversity and abundance of climbers in Budongo Forest Reserve, Uganda. *MSc. Thesis*. Kampala: Makerere University.

Babweteera, F., Plumptre, A. J., and Obua, J. (2000). Effect of gap size and age on climber abundance and diversity in Budongo Forest Reserve, Uganda. *African Journal of Ecology, 38,* 230-237.

Bataamba, A. M. (1990). The ecology of Raptors in and around the Impenetrable Forest, South-Western Uganda. *MSc. Thesis*. Kampala: Makerere University.

Bearder, S. K. and Martin, R. D. (1979). The Social Organization of a Nocturnal Primate Revealed by Radio Tracking. in C. J. Amlaner Jr., and D.W. Macdonald (Pp. 633-648) *A Handbook on Biotelemetry and Radio Tracking*. Oxford: Pergamon Press.

Binggeli, P. (2003). *Lantana camara*. In S. M. Goodman, and J. P. Benstead (Eds.), *The natural history of Madagascar* (476-478). Chicago: University of Chicago Press.

Bitariho, R., McNeilage, A. J., Babaasa, D., and Barigyira, R. (2006). Plant harvest impacts and sustainability in Bwindi Impenetrable National Park, S.W. Uganda. *African Journal of Ecology, 44,* 14-21.

Boesch, C., and Boesch-Achermann, H. (2000). *The Chimpanzees of the Taï Forest: Behavioural Ecology and Evolution*. Oxford: Oxford University Press.

Britten, R. J. (2002). Divergence between samples of chimpanzee and human DNA sequences is 5%, counting indels. *Proceedings of the National Academy of Sciences, 99,* 13633–13635.

Brownlow, A., Plumptre, A. J., Reynolds, V., and Ward, R. (2001). Sources of variation in nesting behavior of chimpanzees (*Pan troglodytes schweinfurthii*) in the Budongo Forest, Uganda. *American Journal of Primatology, 55,* 49-55.

Butynski, T. M. (1984). *Ecological survey of the Impenetrable (Bwindi) Forest*, Uganda, and Recommendations for its Conservation and Management. New York: New York Zoological Society.

Butynski, T. M. (1990). Comparative ecology of blue monkeys (*Cercopithecus mitis*) in high- and low-density subpopulations. *Ecological Monographs, 60,* 1-26.

Byaruhanga, A., Kasoma, P., and Pomeroy, D. (2001). *Important Bird Areas in Uganda. East Africa Natural History Society*, Kampala.

Chalmers, N. R. (1968). Group composition, Ecology and daily activities of free-living mangabeys in Uganda. *Folia Primatologica, 8,* 247-262.

Chapman, C. A., Chapman, L. J., and Wrangham, R. W. (1991). Ugandan elephants help maintain a useful tree. *Agroforestry Today, 3,* 15.

Chapman, C. A., and Wrangham, R. W. (1993). Range use of the forest chimpanzees of Kibale: Implications for the understanding of chimpanzee social organization. *American Journal of Primatology, 31,* 263-273.

Chapman, C. A., and Chapman, L. J. (1994a). Survival without seed dispersers: seedling recruitment under parents. *Conservation Biology, 3,* 675-678.

Chapman, C. A., and Chapman, L. J. (1994b). Observations on synchronous air-breathing in *Clarias. Copeia 1994,* 246-249.

Chapman, C. A. (1995). Primate seed dispersal: coevolution and conservation implications. *Evolutionary Anthropology, 4,* 74-82.

Chapman, C. A., and Chapman, L. J. (1996). Mixed species primate groups in the Kibale forest: Ecological constraints on association. *International Journal of Primatology, 17,* 31-50.

Chapman, C. A., and Chapman, L. J. (1997). Forest Regeneration in Logged and Unlogged Forests of Kibale National Park, Uganda. *Biotropica, 29,* 396-412.

Chapman, C. A., Chapman, L. J., Wrangham, R. W., Isabirye-Basuta, G., and Ben-David, K. (1997). Spatial and temporal availability in the structure of a tropical forest. *African Journal of Ecology, 35,* 287-302.

Chapman, C. A., and Onderdonk, D. A. (1998). Forests without primates: primate/plant codependency. *American Journal of Primatology, 45,* 127-141.

Chapman, C. A., Wrangham, R. W., Chapman, L. J., Kennard, D. K., and Zanne, A. E. (1999). Fruit and flower phenology at two sites in Kibale National Park, Uganda. *Journal of Tropical Ecology, 15,* 189-211.

Chapman, C. A., and Chapman, L. J. (2000). Interdemic variation in mixed-species patterns: common diurnal primates of Kibale National Park, Uganda. *Behavioral Ecology and Sociobiology, 47,* 129-139.

Chapman, C. A., and Lambert, J. E. (2000). Habitat alteration and the conservation of African primates: Case study of Kibale National Park, Uganda. *American Journal of Primatology, 50,* 169-185.

Chapman, C. A., Balcomb, S. R., Gillespie, T. R., Skorupa, J. P., and Struhsaker, T. T. (2000). Long-Term Effects of Logging on African Primate Communities: a 28-Year Comparison From Kibale National Park, Uganda. *Conservation Biology, 14,* 207-217.

Chapman, C. A., Chapman, L. J., and Gillespie, T. R. (2002a). Scale issues in the study of primate foraging: red colobus of Kibale National Park. *American Journal of Physical Anthropology, 117*, 349-363.

Chapman, C. A., Chapman, L. J., Zanne, A., and Burgess. M. A. (2002b). Does weeding promote regeneration of an indigenous tree community in felled pine plantations in Uganda? *Restoration Ecology, 10*, 408-415.

Chapman, C. A., and Chapman, L. J. (2003). Fragmentation and alteration of seed dispersal processes: an initial evaluation of dung beetles, seed fate, seedling diversity. *Biotropica, 35*, 382-393.

Chapman, C. A., Struhsaker, T. T., Lambert, J. E. (2003a). Thirty years of research in Kibale National Park, Uganda reveals a complex picture for conservation. *International Journal of Primatology, 26*, 539-555.

Chapman, C. A., Chapman, L. J., Rode, K. D., Hauck, E. M., and McDowell, L. R. (2003b). Variation in the nutritional value of primate foods: Among trees, time periods, and areas. *International Journal of Primatology, 24*, 317-333.

Chapman, C. A. and Chapman, L. J. (2004). Unfavorable successional pathways and the conservation value of logged tropical forest. *Biodiversity and Conservation, 13*, 2089-2105.

Chapman, C. A., Chapman, L. J., Naughton-Treves, L., Lawes, M. J., and McDowell, L. R. (2004). Predicting folivorous primate abundance: variation of a nutritional model. *American Journal of Primatology, 62*, 55-69.

Chapman, C. A., Lawes, M. J., and Eeley, H. A. C. (2006a). What hope for African primate diversity? *African Journal of Ecology, 44*, 116-133.

Chapman, C. A., Wasserman, M. D., Gillespie, T. R., Speirs, M. L., Lawes, M. J., Saj, T. L., and Ziegler, T. E. (2006b). Do food availability, parasitism, and stress have synergistic effects on red colobus populations living in forest fragments? *American Journal of Physical Anthropology, 131*, 525-534.

Chapman, C. A., Saj, T. L., and Snaith, T. V. (2007) Temporal dynamics of nutrition, parasitism, and stress in colobus monkeys: implications for population regulation and conservation. *American Journal of Physical Anthropology. 134*, 240-250.

Chapman, C. A., Chapman, L. J., Omeja, P. A., and Twinomugisha, D. (2008). Long term studies reveal conservation potential for integrating habitat restoration and animal distribution In R. Wrangham, and E. Ross (Eds.), *Science and Conservation in African Forests* (Pp. 51-74). Cambridge: Cambridge University Press.

Chapman, L. J., and Chapman, C. A. (2001). Tropical forest degradation and aquatic ecosystems: Our current state of knowledge. In M. J. Collares-Pereira,

M. M. Coelho, and L. G. Cowx (Eds.): *Conservation of Freshwater Fishes*: Options for the Future (Pp 237-249). Oxford: Blackwell Science.

Chapman, L. J., and Chapman, C. A. (2003). Fishes of the African rain forests: Emerging and potential threats to a little-known fauna. In T. L. Crisman, L. J. Chapman, C. A. Chapman, and L. S. Kaufman (Eds.), *Conservation, Ecology, and Management of African Freshwaters* (Pp. 176-209). Gainesville: University Press of Florida.

Chapman, L. J., Schneider, K. R., Apodaca, C., and Chapman, C. A. (2004). Respiratory ecology of macroinvertebrates in a swamp-river system of East Africa. *Biotropica, 36*, 572-585.

Chiyo, P. I., Cochrane, E. P., Naughton, L., and Basuta, G. I. (2005). Temporal patterns of crop raiding by elephants: a response to changes in forage quality or crop availability? *African Journal of Ecology, 43*, 48-55.

Choo, G. M., Waterman, P. G., McKey, D. B., and Gartlan, J. S. (1981). A simple enzyme assay for dry matter digestibility and its value in studying food selection by generalist herbivores. *Oecologia, 49*, 170-178.

Clark, A. B. (1985). Sociality in a nocturnal "solitary" prosimian: *Galago crassicaudatus. International Journal of Primatology, 6*, 581-600.

Clark, A. P., and Wrangham, R. W. (1994). Chimpanzee pant hoots: Do they signify food or status? *International Journal of Primatology, 15*, 185-205.

Cochrane, E. P. (2001). Elephants as seed dispersal agents for tropical forest tree species in Kibale National Park, Uganda. *Ph.D. Thesis*. Madison: University of Wisconsin.

Cochrane, E. P. (2003). The need to be eaten: *Balanites wilsoniania* with and without elephant seed-dispersal. *Journal of Tropical Ecology, 19*, 579-589.

Conklin, N. L., and Wrangham, R. W. (1994). The value of figs to a hind-gut fermenting frugivore: a nutritional analysis. *Biochemical Systematics and Ecology, 22*, 137-151.

Cunningham, A. B (1996). People, park and plant use: recommendations for multiple-use zones and development alternatives around Bwindi Impenetrable National Park, Uganda. *People and Plants Working Paper 4.*

Dawkins, H. C. (1955). The refining of mixed forest: a new objective for tropical silviculture. *Empire Forestry Review, 34,* 188-191.

Dominy, N. and Duncan, B. (2005). Seed-spitting Primates and the Conservation and Dispersion of Large-seeded Trees. *International Journal of Primatology, 26,* 631-649.

Dranzoa, C. (1995). Bird populations of primary and logged forests in the Kibale Forest National Park, Uganda. *Ph.D. Thesis*. Kampala: Makerere University.

Dranzoa, C. (2001). Breeding birds in the tropical rain forests of Kibale National Park, Uganda *African Journal of Ecology, 39*, 74–82.

Duncan, R. S. and Chapman, C. A. (1999). Seed dispersal and potential forest succession in abandoned agriculture in tropical Africa. *Ecological Applications, 9*, 998-1008.

Duncan, R. S., and Chapman, C. A. (2003a). Consequences of plantation harvest during tropical forest restoration in Uganda. *Forest Ecology and Management, 173*, 235-250.

Duncan, R. S., and Chapman, C. A. (2003b). Tree-shrub interactions during early forest succession in Uganda. *Restoration Ecology, 11*, 198-207.

Efitre, J. (2000). *Preliminary assessment of water quality of rivers draining Bwindi Impenetrable National Park (BINP), South-Western Uganda.* Institute of Tropical Forest Conservation Report.

Eggeling, W. J. (1947). *Forestry working plan for the Budongo and Siba Forests, 1945-1954.* Uganda Forestry Department and Commonwealth Secretariat.

Eilu, G., Hafashimana, D. L. N. and Kasenene, J. M. (2004). Tree species distribution in forests of the Albertine Rift, Western Uganda. *African Journal of Ecology, 42*, 100-110.

Eltringham, S. K. (1974). Changes in the large mammal community of Mweya Peninsula, Rwenzori National Park, Uganda, following removal of hippopotamus. *Journal of Applied Ecology, 11*, 855-865.

Eltringham, S. K. and Malpas, R. C (1993). The conservation status of Uganda's game and forest reserves in 1982 and 1983. *African Journal of Ecology, 31*, 91-105.

Estes, R. D. (1991). *The Behavior Guide to African Mammals: Including Hoofed Mammals, Carnivores, Primates.* University of California Press.

Fairgrieve, C. (1995). The comparative ecology of blue monkeys (*Cercopithecus mitis stuhlmannii*) in logged and unlogged forest, Budongo Forest Reserve, Uganda: the effects of logging on habitat and population density. *Ph.D. Thesis.* Edinburgh: The University of Edinburgh.

Fawcett, K. A. (2000). Female relationships and food availability in a forest community of chimpanzees. *Ph.D. Thesis.* Edinburgh: University of Edinburgh.

Fimbel, R. A. and Fimbel, C. C. (1996). The role of exotic conifer plantations in rehabilitating degraded tropical forest lands: A case study from the Kibale Forest in Uganda. *Forest Ecology and Management, 81*, 215-226.

Forest Department (1996a). Mt Elgon National Park. *Biodiversity Report Series, Report No. 1.* P. Howard, T. Davenport and M. Baltzer (Eds.). Kampala: Forest Department.

Forest Department (1996b). Rwenzori Mountains. *Biodiversity Report Series, Report No. 2.* P. Howard, T. Davenport, and M. Baltzer (Eds.). Kampala: Forest Department.

Forest Department (1996c). Budongo Forest Reserve. *Biodiversity Report Series, Report No. 3.* P. Howard, T. Davenport, and R. Mathews (Eds.). Kampala: Forest Department.

Forest Department (1996d). Kibale Forest. *Biodiversity Report Series, Report No. 5.* P. Howard, T. Davenport, and R. Mathews (Eds.). Kampala: Forest Department.

Forest Department (1996e). Semliki Forest. *Biodiversity Report Series, Report No. 15.* T. Davenport, and P. Howard (Eds). Kampala: Forest Department.

Forest Department (1996f). Bwindi Impenetrable National Park. *Biodiversity Report Series, Report No. 19.* T. Davenport, P. Howard, and R. Mathews (Eds.). Kampala: Forest Department.

Forest Department (2002). *Uganda Forestry and Nature Conservation Master Plan.* Kampala: Ministry of Lands and Environment. Kampala: Forest Department.

Garner, K. J., and Ryder, O. A. (1996). Mitochondrial DNA Diversity in Gorillas. *Molecular Phylogenetics and Evolution, 6,* 39-48.

Gartlan, J. S., McKey, D. B. Waterman, P. G., Mbi, C. N., and Struhsaker, T. T. (1980). A comparative study of the phytochemistry of two African rainforests. *Biochemical Systematics and Ecology, 8,* 401-422.

GEF (1995). *Bwindi Impenetrable National Park and Mgahinga Gorilla National Park Conservation.* Project document.

Ghiglieri, J. P., Butynski, T. M., Struhsaker, T. T., Leland, L., Wallis, S. J. and Waser, P. (1982). Bush pig, *Potamochoerus porcus,* polychromatism and ecology in Kibale Forest, Uganda. *African Journal of Ecology, 20,* 231-236.

Ghiglieri, M. (1985). The social ecology of chimpanzees. *Scientific American, 252,* 84-91.

Gillespie, T., Greiner, E. C. and Chapman, C. A. (2005). Gastrointestinal parasites of the colobus monkeys of Uganda. *Journal of Parasitology 91,* 569-573.

Gillespie, T., and Chapman, C. A. (2006). Forest fragment attributes predict parasite infection dynamics in primate metapopulations. *Conservation Biology, 20,* 441-448.

Gillespie, T. R. and Chapman, C. A. (2008) Forest Fragmentation, the Decline of an Endangered Primate, and Changes in Host–Parasite Interactions Relative to an Unfragmented Forest. *American Journal of Primatology, 70,* 222-230.

Goldberg, T., Gillespie, T. R., and Rwego, I. B. (2008). Health and disease in the people, primates, and domestic animals of Kibale National Park: Implications for Conservation. In In R. Wrangham, and E. Ross (Eds.). *Science and Conservation in African Forests* (Pp. 75-87). Cambridge: Cambridge University Press.

Goldman, A., Hartter, J., Southworth, J., and Binford, M. (2008). The human landscape around the Island Park: impacts and responses to Kibale National park In R. Wrangham, and E. Ross (Eds.). *Science and Conservation in African Forests* (Pp 129-144). Cambridge: Cambridge University Press.

Goldsmith, M. (2001). *Sympatric Ecology of Chimpanzees and Mountain Gorillas in Bwindi Impenetrable National Park. A report* to UWA.

Goldsmith, M. L., Glick, J., and Ngabirano, E. (2006). Gorillas living on the edge: literally and figuratively. In N. E. Newton-Fisher, H. Notman, J. D. Paterson, and V. Reynolds (Eds.). *Primates of Western Uganda* (Pp. 405-422). New York: Springer.

Grove, S. (1995). *A nature conservation source-book for forestry professionals.* Commonwealth Secretariat and Uganda Forestry Department.

Groves, C. (2007). The endemic Uganda mangabey, *Lophocebus ugandae*, and other members of the albigena-Group (*Lophocebus*). *Primate Conservation, 22*, 123-128.

Guschanski, K., Vigilant, L., McNeilage, A., Gray, M., Kagoda, E., and Robbins, M.M. 2009. Counting elusive animals: comparing field and genetic census of the entire mountain gorilla population of Bwindi Impenetrable National Park, Uganda. *Biological Conservation*, 142, 290-300

Hamilton, A., Cunningham, A., Byarugaba, D. and Kayanja, F. (2000). Conservation in a Region of Political Instability: Bwindi Impenetrable Forest, Uganda. *Conservation Biology*, 14, 1722-1725.

Harris, C. M. (1934). *Provisional working plan report for the Bunyoro Forests, Uganda.* Kampala: Uganda Forest Department.

Hashimoto, C. (1995). Population census of the chimpanzees in the Kalinzu Forest, Uganda: Comparison between methods with nest counts. *Primates, 36*, 477-488.

Hauser, M. D., and Wrangham, R. W. (1990). Recognition of predator and competitor calls in nonhuman primates and birds: a preliminary report. *Ethology, 86,* 116-130.

Hill, C. M. (1997). Crop-raiding by wild vertebrates: the farmer's perspective in an agricultural community in western Uganda. *International Journal of Pest Management, 43,* 77-84.

Hill, C., Osborn, F. and Plumptre, A. J. (2002). Human-Wildlife Conflict: Identifying the problem and possible solutions. *Albertine Rift Technical Report Series* Vol. 1. Wildlife Conservation Society.

Hladik, C. M. (1979). Diet and ecology of prosimians. In G. A. Doyle, and R. D. Martin. *The Study of Prosimian Behavior*. New York: Academic Press.

Howard, P. C. (1991). Nature Conservation in Uganda's Tropical Forest Reserves. IUCN, Gland, Switzerland and Cambridge, U.K.

Huffman, M. A., and Wrangham, R. W. (1994). Diversity of medicinal plant use by chimpanzees in wild chimpanzees. In R. W. Wrangham, W. C. McGrew, F. B. de Waal, and P. G. Heltne (Eds.), Chimpanzee Cultures (Pp. 129-148). Cambridge: Harvard University Press.

Hulme, M., Doherty, R., Ngara, T., New, M., and Lister, D. (2001). African Climate Change: 1900-2100. *Climate Research*, 17, 145-168.

Intergovernmental Panel on Climate Change (IPCC) (2001). The Scientific Basis. *Contribution of Working Group I to the Third Assessment Report of the Intergovernmental Panel on Climate Change*. J.T. Houghton, Y. Ding, D.J. Griggs, M. Noguer, P.J. van der Linden, X. Dai, K. Maskell, and C.A. Johnson, (Eds). Cambridge, United Kingdom and New York, NY: Cambridge University Press.

Isabirye-Basuta, G. (1989). Feeding ecology of chimpanzees in the Kibale Forest, Uganda. In P. N. Heltne, and L. Marquardt (Eds.), *Understanding Chimpanzees* (Pp 116-127). Cambridge: Harvard University Press.

Isabirye-Basuta, G. (1990). The ecology and conservation status of the chimpanzee *Pan troglodytes* Blumenbach) in Kibale Forest. *Ph.D. Thesis*. Kampala: Makerere Universty.

IUCN (1994a). World Heritage Nomination, Bwindi Impenetrable National Park. Summary prepared by *IUCN/WCMC* based on documentation submitted by the Government of Uganda.

IUCN (1994b). World Heritage Nomination, Rwenzori National Park. Summary prepared by *IUCN/WCMC* based on documentation submitted by the Government of Uganda.

Kahindo, C. (2000). Bird communities in gaps of Budongo Forest Reserve, Uganda. *MSc. Thesis*, Kampala: Makerere University.

Kalema, G. et al. (1998) An outbreak of sarcoptic mange in free-ranging mountain gorillas (*Gorilla gorilla beringei*) in Bwindi Impenetrable National Park, South Western Uganda. Proceedings of the Joint Conference of American Association of Zoo Veterinarians/ American Association of Wildlife Veterinarians (Pp. 438).

Kalema-Zikusoka, G., Kock, R. A., and Macfie, E. J. (2002). Scabies in free-ranging mountain gorillas (*Gorilla gorilla beringei*) in Bwindi Impenetrable National Park, Uganda. *Veterinary Record, 150,* 12–15.

Kalina, J. (1988). Ecology and behavior of the black-and-white casqued hornbill (*Bycanistes subcylindricus subquadratus*) in Kibale Forest, Uganda. *Ph.D. Thesis*, Lansing: Michigan State University.

Kalina, J. (1991). Mgahinga Gorilla National Park. *Reference for management*. Report to the Uganda Government.

Kasangaki, A., Babaasa, D. Bitariho, R., and Mugiri, G. (2001). *A survey of burnt areas in Bwindi Impenetrable and Mgahinga Gorilla National Parks, S.W. Uganda: The fires of 2000*. Institute of Tropical Forest Conservation Report, Ecological Monitoring Program.

Kasangaki, A., Babaasa, D., Efitre, J., McNeilage, A., and Bitariho, R. (2006). Links between anthropogenic perturbations and benthic macroinvertebrate assemblages in Afromontane forest streams of Uganda. *Hydrobiologia, 563*, 231-245.

Kasenene, J. M. (1984). The influence of selective logging on rodent populations and the regeneration of selected tree species in the Kibale Forest, Uganda. *Tropical Ecology, 25*, 179-195.

Kasenene, J. M. (1987). The influence of mechanized selective logging, felling intensity and gap-size on the regeneration of a tropical moist forest in the Kibale Forest Reserve, Uganda. *Ph.D. Thesis*. East Lansing: Michigan State University.

Kasenene, J. M. (1998). Forest association and phenology of wild coffee in Kibale National Park, Uganda. *African Journal of Ecology, 36*, 241-250.

Kasenene, J. M., and Ross, E. A. (2008). Community benefits from long-term research programs: a case study from Kibale National Park, Uganda. In R. Wrangham, and E. Ross (Eds.). *Science and Conservation in African Forests* (Pp. 99-114). Cambridge: Cambridge University Press.

Kingdon, J. (1967). Working *plan for Mgahinga Central Forest Reserve, Kigezi District, Uganda (1967-1977)*. Report to the Forest Department.

Kingdon, J. (1974). *East African Mammals*. V.1. Chicago: University of Chicago Press.

Kingston, B. (1967). *Working plan for Kibale and Itwara Central Forest Reserves*. Entebbe: Uganda Forest Department.

Krishnamani, R., and Mahaney, W. C. (2000). Geophagy among primates: Adaptive significance and ecological consequences. *Animal Behavior, 59*, 899-915.

Lambert, J. E. (1998). Primate frugivory in Kibale National Park, Uganda, and its implications for human use of forest resources. *African Journal of Ecology, 36*, 243-240.

Lambert, J. E. (2001). Redtailed guenons (*Cercopithecus ascanius*) and *Strychnos mitis*: Evidence for plant benefits beyond seed dispersal. *International Journal of Primatology, 22*, 189-201.

Lamprey, R., Buhanga, E., and Omoding, J. (2003). A study of wildlife distributions, wildlife management systems, and options for wildlife-based livelihoods in Uganda. *A report for IFPRI (International Food Policy Research Institute)/USAID*. Kampala, Uganda.

Lang Brown, J. R., and Harrop, J. F. (1962). The ecology and soils of the Kibale grasslands, Uganda. *East African Agricultural and Forestry Journal, 17,* 264-272.

Langdale-Brown, I., Osmaston, H. A., and Wilson, J. G. (1964). *The Vegetation Uganda and its bearing on Land Use.* Entebbe: Government of Uganda Printer.

Laporte, N., Walker, W., Stabach, J., and Landsberg, F. (2008). *Monitoring forest-savanna dynamics in Kibale National Park with satellite imagery (1989-2003): implications for the management of wildlife habitat.* In R. Wrangham, and E. Ross, (Eds.), Science and Conservation in African Forests (Pp. 38-50). Cambridge: Cambridge University Press.

Lawes, M. J., and Chapman, C. A. (2006). Does the herb *Acanthus pubescens* and/or elephants suppress tree regeneration in disturbed Afrotropical forest? *Forest Ecology and Management, 221*, 278-284.

Laws, R. M., Parker, I. S. C., and Johnstone, R. C. B. (1975). *Elephants and their habitats: the ecology of elephants in North Bunyoro, Uganda.* Oxford: Clarendon Press.

Leggat, G. J., and Beaton, A. (1961). *Forestry working plan for the Ruwenzori Central Forest Reserves, First Revision, 1961-1971.* Kampala: Uganda Forestry Department and Commonwealth Secretariat.

Leggat, G.J. and H.A. Osmaston (1961). *Forestry working plan for the Impenetrable Central Forest Reserve Kigezi District, 1961-1971.* Kampala: Uganda Forestry Department and Commonwealth Secretariat.

Lejju, J. B., Oryem-Origa, H., and Kasenene, J. M. (2001). Regeneration of indigenous trees in Mgahinga Gorilla National Park, Uganda. *African Journal of Ecology, 39*, 65-73.

Leland, L., and Struhsaker, T. T. (1987). Monkey business. *Animal Kingdom, 90*, 24-37.

Lwanga, J. S. (1994). The role of seed and seedling predators and browsers in the regeneration of two forest canopy species (*Mimusops bagshawei* and *Strombosia scheffleri*) in Kibale Forest Reserve, Uganda. *Ph.D. Dissertation*, Gainesville: University of Florida.

Lwanga, J. S., Butynski, T. M., Struhsaker, T. T. (2000). Tree population dynamics in Kibale National Park, Uganda 1975–1998. *African Journal of Ecology, 38*, 1365-2028.

Lwanga, J. S. (2003). Forest succession in Kibale National Park, Uganda: implications for forest restoration and management. *African Journal of Ecology, 41*, 9-22.

Lwanga, J. S. (2006). Spatial distribution of primates in a mosaic of colonizing and old growth forest at Ngogo, Kibale National Park, Uganda. *International Journal of Primatology, 47*, 230-238.

Mahaney, W. C., Milner, M. W., Sanmugadas, K., Hancock, R. G. V. Aufreiter, S., Wrangham, R. W., and Pier, H. W. (1997). Analysis of geophagy soils in Kibale Forest, Uganda. *Primates, 38*,159-176.

Makanga, S. (2002). Health risks of the Mountain Gorilla from rodents and man's influence on rodent dynamics within and around Bwindi Impenetrable National Park, Southwestern Uganda. *MSc dissertation*. Kampala: Makerere University.

Makanga, S., Bwangamoi, O., Nizeyi, J. B., Crafield, M., and Dranzoa, C. (2004). Parasites found in rodents in Bwindi Impenetrable National Park, Uganda. *African Journal of Ecology, 42*, 78-81.

McCoy, J. (1995). Responses of blue and red duikers to logging in the Kibale Forest of Western Uganda. *MSc Thesis*. Gainesville: University of Florida.

McNeilage, A., Plumptre, A., Brock-Doyle, A., and Vedder, A., (1998). Bwindi Impenetrable National Park, Uganda Gorilla and Large Mammal Census, 1997. *Wildlife Conservation Society Working paper No. 14.*

McNeilage, A., Robbins, M. M., Gray, M., Olupot, W., Babaasa, D., Bitariho, R., Kasangaki, A., Rainer, H., Asuma, S., Mugiri, G., and Baker, J. (2006). Census of the mountain gorilla *Gorilla beringei beringei* population in Bwindi Impenetrable National Park, Uganda. *Oryx, 40*, 419-427.

Mileham, L., Taylor, R. G., Fischer, A., Osmaston, H., Kaser, G., Nakileza, B., and Tindimugaya, C. (In prep). Recent evidence of continued deglaciation in the Ruwenzori mountains of Uganda: application of optical spaceborn imagery.

Mitani, J. C., Struhsaker, T. T., and Lwanga, J. S. (2000). Primate community dynamics in old growth forest over 23.5 years at Ngogo, Kibale National Park, Uganda: implications for conservation and census methods. *International Journal of Primatology, 21*, 269-286.

Mitani, J. C., Sanders, W. J., Lwanga, J. S., and Windfelder, T. S. (2001). Predatory behaviour of crowned-hawk eagles (*Stephanoaetus coronatus*) in

Kibale National Park, Uganda. *Behavioural Ecology and Sociobiology, 49*, 187-195.

Mitchell, B. L. (1961). Ecological aspects of game control measures in African wilderness and forested areas. *Kirkia, 1*, 120-128.

Moore, K. (1998). *A plague of plants*. Wildlands Restoration Team. 22pp.

Mugisha, A., Jacobson, S. K., Alavalapati, J., and Chapman, C. A. (In prep). Community-based conservation programs in Uganda- providing benefits?

Mugisha, L. (2004). A survey of gastrointestinal parasites of habituated wild chimpanzees (*Pan troglodytes*), humans and rodents in Budongo Forest Reserve. *MSc. Thesis*. Kampala: Makerere University.

Mugisha, A. (2008). Potential interactions of research with the development and management of ecotourism. In R. Wrangham and E. Ross (Eds.) *Science and Conservation in African Forests* (Pp. 115-128). Cambridge: Cambridge University Press.

Muller, M. (2002). Agonistic relations among Kanyawara chimpanzees. In: C. Boesch, G. Hohmann, and L. F. Marchant (Eds.) *Behavioural Diversity in Chimpanzees and Bonobos* (Pp. 112-124). Cambridge: Cambridge University Press.

Musamali, P. (1996). The ecology, diversity and relative abundance of small mammals in primary and disturbed forest compartments in the Budongo Forest Reserve. *MSc. Thesis*. Kampala: Makerere University.

Musinguzi, J. (2004). The impact of fire on the forest dynamics in Bwindi Impenetrable National Park, Southwestern Uganda. *MSc. Thesis*. Mbarara: Mbarara University of Science and Technology.

Muyambi, F. (2004). Assessment of impact of tourism on the behaviours of mountain gorillas in Bwindi Impenetrable National Park. *MSc. Thesis*. Kampala: Makerere University.

Mwandha, J. S., Langoya, C. D. and Kasoma, P. M. B. (2003). The state of protected areas in Uganda. In A. Roberts (ed.), *Protected Areas in Uganda, Benefits Beyond Boundaries*. Kampala: Acha Graphics.

Mwima, P.M, Obua, J., and Oryem-Origa, H. (2001). Effect of logging on the natural regeneration of *Khaya anthotheca* in Budongo Forest Reserve, Uganda. *Internat. Forestry Review, 3*, 131-135.

Mwima, P. M. and McNeilage, A. J (2003). Natural regeneration and ecological recovery in Bwindi Impenetrable National Park, Uganda. *African Journal of Ecology 41*, 93-98.

Namara, A., McNeilage, A. J., Franks, P., Blomley, T., Infield, M., Malpas, R., Donaldson, A., and Olupot, W. In Progress. Bwindi and Mgahinga National

Parks in Uganda: has 15 years of ICD programming succeeded in increasing support for conservation among local communities?

Nangendo, G., van Straaten, O., and de Gier, A. (2005). Biodiversity conservation through burning: a case study of woodlands in Budongo Forest Reserve, N.W. Uganda. M. A. F. Ros-Tonen, T. Dietz (Eds.), *African Forests between Nature and Livelihood Resources: Interdisciplinary Studies in Conservation and Forest Management* (Pp. 113-128). New York: The Edwin Mellen Press, Lewiston.

Nangendo, G., A. Skidmore, A. K., and van Oosten, H. (2007). Mapping east African tropical forests and woodlands – a comparison of classifiers. *ISPRS Journal of Photogrammetry and Remote Sensing, 61*, 393-404.

Naughton-Treves, L. (1997). Farming the forest edge: Vulnerable places and people around Kibale National Park. *The Geographical Review, 87*, 27-46.

Naughton-Treves, L., Treves, A., Chapman, C. A., and Wrangham. R. (1998) Temporal patterns of crop-raiding by primates: linking food availability in croplands and adjacent forest. *Journal of Applied Ecology, 35,* 596–606.

Naughton-Treves, L., and Chapman, C. A. (2002). Fuelwood resources and forest regeneration on fallow land in Uganda. *Journal of Sustainable Forestry, 14*, 19-32.

Ndagalasi, H.J., Bitariho, R., and Dovie, D. B. K. (2007). Harvesting of non-timber products and implications for conservation in two montane forests of East Africa. *Biological Conservation. 134,* 242-250.

Newton-Fisher, N. E. (2003). The home range of the Sonso community of chimpanzees from the Budongo Forest, Uganda. *African Journal of Ecology, 41*, 150-156.

Nizeyi, J., Cranfield, M., and Graczyk, T. (2004). Cattle near the Bwindi Impenetrable National Park, Uganda, as a reservoir of *Cryptosporidium parvum* and *Giardia duodenalis* for local community and free-ranging gorillas. *Parasitology Research, 88,* 380-385.

Nkurunungi, J. B. (2003). The availability and distribution of fruit and non-fruit plant resources in Bwindi: Their influence on gorilla habitat use and food choice. *Ph.D. Thesis.* Kampala: Makerere University.

Nkurunungi, J. B., Ganas, J., Robbins, M. M., and Stanford, C. B. (2004). A comparison of two mountain gorilla habitats in Bwindi Impenetrable National Park, Uganda. *African Journal of Ecology, 42*, 289-297.

Nummelin, M., and Hanski, I. (1989). Dung beetles of the Kibale Forest, Uganda: comparison between virgin and managed forests. *Journal of Tropical Ecology, 5,* 349-352.

Nummelin, M. (1990). Relative habitat use of duikers, bushpigs, and elephants in virgin and selectively logged areas of the Kibale Forest, Uganda. *Tropical Zoology 3*:, 111-120.

Nummelin, M. and Borowiec, L. (1991). Cassidinae beetles of the Kibale Forest, Western Uganda; comparison between virgin and managed forests. *African Journal of Ecology, 29*, 10-17.

Oates, J. F. (1977a). The Guereza and man: How man has affected the distribution and abundance of *Colobus guereza* and other black colobus monkeys. In Prince Rainier III and G.H. Bourne (Eds) *Primate Conservation* (Pp. 419-467). London: Academic Press.

Oates, J. F. (1977b). The Guereza and its food. In T. H. Clutton-Brock (Ed.), *Primate Ecology: Studies of feeding and ranging behaviour in lemurs, monkeys and apes* (Pp 275-321). Academic press, London.

Oates, J. F. (1978). Water plant and soil consumption by guereza monkeys (*Colobus guereza*): A relationship with minerals and toxins in the diet. *Biotropica, 10*, 241-253.

Ocen, M. 2000. The status and ecology of duikers, Cephalophus spp. at Mgahinga Gorilla National Park. *MSc. Thesis*. Kampala: Makerere University.

Okecha, A. A. and Newton-Fisher, N. E. (2006). The diet of olive baboons (*Papio anubis*) in Budongo Forest Reserve, Uganda. In N. E. Newton-Fisher, H. Notman, J.D. Paterson, and V. Reynolds (Eds.). *Primates of Western Uganda* (Pp. 61-73).. New York: Springer.

Olupot, W., Chapman, C. A., Brown, C. H. and Waser, P. M. (1994). Mangabey (*Cercocebus albigena*) population density, group size, and ranging: a twenty-year comparison. *American Journal of Primatology, 32*, 197-205.

Olupot, W. 1998. Long-term variation in mangabey (*Cercocebus albigena johnstoni* Lydekker) feeding in Kibale National Park, Uganda. *African Journal of Ecology, 36*, 96-101.

Olupot, W., Waser, P. M. and Chapman, C. A. (1998). Mangabey (*Lophocebus albigena*) fruit finding: Are monitoring of fig trees and use of sympatric loud frugivore calls possible strategies? *International Journal of Primatology, 19*, 339-353.

Olupot, W. (1999). Mangabey dispersal and conservation in Kibale National Park, Uganda. *Ph.D. Thesis*. West Lafayette, Indiana: Purdue University.

Olupot, W. (2000). Body mass differences among male mangabeys inhabiting logged and unlogged forest compartments. *Conservation Biology, 11*, 843-853.

Olupot, W. and Waser, P. M. (2001a). Correlates of intergroup transfer in male grey-cheeked mangabeys. *International Journal of Primatology, 22*, 169-187.

Olupot, W. and Waser, P. M. (2001). Activity patterns, habitat use and mortality risks of mangabey males living outside social groups. *Animal Behaviour, 61,* 1227-1235.

Olupot, W. (2004). Boundary edge effects in Bwindi Impenetrable National Park, Uganda. *Institute of Tropical Forest Conservation,* A report.

Olupot, W. and P.M. Waser (2005) Patterns of male residency and intergroup transfer in grey-cheeked mangabeys (*Lophocebus albigena*). *American Journal of Primatology 66,* 331-349.

Olupot, W., McNeilage, A. J. and Plumptre, A. J. (2008). Constraints to sustainability of benefits from wildlife resources: an analysis of socioeconomics of bushmeat hunting in and around major hunting sites in Uganda. *A report to USAID/PRIME-West Project.*

Olupot, W. and Plumptre, A. J. (2008). The use of research: how long term research in Uganda's National Parks has been used. In R. Wrangham and E. Ross (Eds.) Science and Conservation in African Forests (Pp. 15-26). Cambridge, Cambridge University Press.

Olupot, W., (2009). A variable edge effect on trees of Bwindi Impenetrable National Park, Uganda, and its bearing on measurement parameters. *Biological Conservation 142,* 789-797.

Olupot, W., Barigyira, R. and Chapman, C. A. (2009a). The status of anthropogenic threat at the people-park interface of Bwindi Impenetrable National Park, Uganda. *Environmental Conservation, 36,* 41–50.

Olupot, W., Barigyira, R. and McNeilage, A. J. (2009b). Edge-related variation in medicinal and other 'useful' wild plants of Bwindi Impenetrable National Park, Uganda. *Conservation Biology 23,* 1138-1145.

Olupot, W., and Sheil, D. Evaluating a low cost method for assessing large mammal and bird use of different habitats. A report.

Osborn, F. V. (2004). Seasonal variation of feeding patterns and food selection by crop raiding elephants in Zimbabwe. *African Journal of Ecology, 42,* 322-327.

Osmaston, H. A. (1959). *Working plan for the Kibale and Itwara forests: period 1959–1965.* Entebbe: Government of Uganda Printer.

Osmaston, H. (1998). Exploration, science and conservation on the Rwenzori mountains of the moon. In H. Osmaston, J. Tukahirwa, C. Basalirwa, and J. Nyakaana (Eds.), *The Rwenzori Mountains National Park, Uganda* (Pp. 13-30). Kampala: Makerere University.

Owiunji, I., and Plumptre, A. J. (1998). Bird communities in logged and unlogged compartments in Budongo Forest, Uganda. *Forest Ecology and Management, 108,* 115-126.

Owiunji, I. (2000). Changes in avian communities of Budongo Forest Reserve after 70 years of selective logging. *Ostrich, 71,* 216-219.

Owiunji, I. (2001). Bird recovery in a recently logged forest of Budongo. *Ostrich Supplement No.* 15, 56-59.

Paul, J. R., Randle, A. M., Chapman, C. A., and Chapman, L. J. (2004). Arrested succession in logging gaps: is tree seedling growth and survival limiting? *African Journal of Ecology, 42,* 245-251.

Paterson, J. D. (2006). Aspects of diet, foraging, and seed predation in Ugandan forest baboons. In N. E. Newton-Fisher, H. Notman, J.D. Paterson, and V. Reynolds (Eds.), *Primates of Western Uganda* (Pp. 75-92). New York: Springer.

Pebsworth, P., Krief, S., and Huffman, M. A. (2006). The role of diet in self-medication among chimpanzees in the Sonso and Kanyawara communities, Uganda. In N. E. Newton-Fisher, H. Notman, J. D. Paterson, and V. Reynolds (Eds.). *Primates of Western Uganda* (105-133). New York: Springer.

Plumptre, A. J., and Reynolds V. (1994). The impact of selective logging on the primate populations in the Budongo Forest Reserve, Uganda. *Journal of Applied Ecology, 31,* 631-641.

Plumptre, A. and Reynolds, V. (1996) Censusing chimpanzees in the Budongo forest. *International Journal of Primatology* 17, 85-99.

Plumptre, A. J. (1996). Changes following 60 years of selective timber harvesting in the Budongo Forest Reserve, Uganda. *Forest Ecology and Management, 89,* 101-113.

Plumptre, A. J., Bizumuremyi, J. B., Uwimana, F., and Ndaruhebeye, J. D. (1997a). The effects of the Rwandan civil war on poaching of ungulates in the Parc National des Volcans. *Oryx, 31,* 265-273.

Plumptre, A. J, Reynolds, V., and Bakuneeta, C. (1997b). The effects of selective logging in monodominant tropical forests on biodiversity. *Final report of ODA project number R6057.* Budongo Forest Project, Institute of Biological Anthropology, University of Oxford, 58 Banbury Road, Oxford OX2 6QS, UK.

Plumptre, A., and Owiunji, I. O. (1998). Bird communities in logged and unlogged compartments in Budongo Forest, Uganda. *Forest Ecology and Management, 108,* 115-126.

Plumptre, A. J., Mugume, S., Cox, D., Montgomery, C., (2001). Chimpanzee and large mammal survey of Budongo Forest Reserve and Kibale National Park. *Report to Wildlife Conservation Society.*

Plumptre, A.J., Cox, D., and Mugume, S. (2003a). The Status of Chimpanzees in Uganda. *Albertine Rift Technical Reports,* No. 2.

Plumptre, A. J., Behangana, M., Davenport, T., Kahindo, C., Kityo, R., Ndomba, E., Ssegawa, P., Eilu, G., Nkuutu, D., and Owiunji, I. (2003b). The Biodiversity of the Albertine Rift. *Albertine Rift Technical Reports* No. 3.

Plumptre, A.J., Kayitare, A., Rainer, H., Gray, M., Munanura, I., Barakabuye, N., Asuma, S., Sivha, M., and Namara, A. (2004). The Socio-economic status of people living near protected areas in the Central Albertine Rift. *Albertine Rift Technical Reports,* 4.

Plumptre, A. J. and Cox, D. (2005). Counting primates for conservation: primate surveys in Uganda. *Primates, 47,* 65-73.

Plumptre, A. J. (2006). The diets, preferences, and overlap of the primate community in the Budongo Forest Reserve, Uganda: effects of logging on primate diets. In N. E. Newton-Fisher., H. Notman, J.D. Paterson, and V. Reynolds (Eds.), *Primates of Western Uganda.* (Pp. 345-371). New York: Springer.

Plumptre, A. J., Davenport, T. R. B. Behangana, M., Kityo, R., Eilu, G., Ssegawa, P., Ewango, C., Meirte, D., Kahindo, C., Herremans, M., Peterhans, J. K., Pilgrim, J. D., Wilson, M., Languy, M., Moyer, D. (2007). The biodiversity of the Albertine Rift. *Biological Conservation, 134,* 178-194.

Purna, B. C., Edmund, G., Barrow, C. and Muhweezi, A. (2004). *Securing Protected Area Integrity and Rural People's Livelihoods: Lessons from Twelve Years of the Kibale and Semliki Conservation and Development Project.* Kibale-Semliki Conservation and Development Project.

Reed, M. S. and Clokie, M. R. J. (2000). Effects of grazing and cultivation on forest plant communities in Mt. Elgon National Park, Uganda. *African Journal of Ecology, 38,* 154-162.

Reed, K. E. and Bidner, L. R. (2004). Primate communities: past, present, and possible future. *Yearbook of Physical Anthropology*, 47, 2-39.

Reynolds, V., and Reynolds, F (1965). Chimpanzees of the Budongo Forest. In I. De Vore (Ed.) *Primate Behavior: field studies of monkeys and apes.* New York: Holt, Rinehart and Winston.

Reynolds, V., Plumptre, A. J., Greenham, J. and Harbone, J. (1998). Condensed tannins and sugars in the diet of chimpanzees (*Pan troglodytes scweinfurthii*) in the Budongo Forest, Uganda. *Oecologia, 115,* 331-336.

Reynolds, V., Wallis, J., and Kyamanywa, R. (2003). Fragments, sugar, and chimpanzees in Masindi District, Western Uganda. In L. Marsh (ed), *Primates in Fragments: ecology in conservation* (Pp. 309–320). New York: Kluwer Academic/Plenum Publishers.

Reynolds, V. (2005). The chimpanzees of the Budongo Forest: Ecology, Behaviour, and Conservation. Oxford: Oxford University Press.

Richards, P. W. (1964). *The tropical rainforest: An ecological study.* Cambridge: Cambridge University Press.

Rode, K. D., Chapman, C. A., McDowell, L. R., and Stickler, C. (In Press). Nutritional correlates of population density across habitats and logging intensities in redtail monkeys (*Cercopithecus ascanius*). *Biotropica, 38,* 625-634.

Rodriguez, E., and Wrangham, R. (1993). Zoopharmacognosy: the use of medicinal plants by animals. In K. R. Downum *et al.* (Ed.). *Phytochemical Potential of Tropical Plants*, pp 89-105. New York: Plenum Press.

Rothman, J. M., Bowman, D. D., Kalema-Zikusoka, G., and Nkurunungi, J. B. (2006a). The parasites of the gorillas in Bwindi Impenetrable National Park, Uganda. In Newton-Fisher, N. E., H. Notman, J. D. Paterson, and V. Reynods (Eds.) *Primates of Western Uganda* (Pp. 171-192). New York: Springer.

Rothman J.M., Van Soest, P. J., and Pell, A. N. (2006b). Decaying wood is a sodium source for mountain gorillas. *Biology Letters, 2,* 321-324.

Ruvolo M. (1997). Molecular phylogeny of the hominoids: inferences from multiple independent DNA sequence data sets. *Molecular Biology and Evolution, 14,* 248–265.

Rwego, I. B. (2004). Prevalence of observed clinical signs in Mt. Gorillas of Bwindi Impenetrable National Park, Uganda. *MSc. Dissertation.* Kampala: Makerere University.

Sandbrook, C. and Semple, S. (2006). The rules and the reality of mountain gorilla *Gorilla beringei beringei* tracking: How close do tourists get? *Oryx, 40,* 428-433.

Santiago, M. L., Lukasik, M., Kamenya, S., Li, Y., Bibollet-Ruche, F., Bailes, E., Muller, M. N., Emery, M., Goldenberg, D. A., Lwanga, J. S., Ayouba, A., Nerrienet, E., McClure, H. M., Heeney, J. L., Watts, D. P., Pusey, A. E., Collins, D. A., Wrangham, R. W., Goodall, J., Brookfield, J. F., Sharp, P. M., Shaw, G. M., and Hahn, B. H. (2003). Foci of endemic simian immunodeficiency virus infection in wild-living eastern chimpanzees (*Pan troglodytes schweinfurthii*). *Journal of Virology, 77,* 7545-62.

Sarmiento, E. E., Butynski, T. M., and Kalina, J. (1996). Gorillas of Bwindi-Impenetrable Forest and the Virunga Volcanoes: taxonomic implications of morphological and ecological differences. *American Journal of Primatology, 40,* 1-21.

Schmitz, D. C., and Simberloff, D. (1997). Biological Invasions: A Growing Threat. Issues in Science and Technology. Available from: http://www.nap.edu/issues/13.4/schmit.htm.

Seavy, N. E., Apodaca, C. K., and Balcomb, S. (2001). Associations of Crested Guineafowl *Guttera pucherani* and monkeys in Kibale National Park. *Ibis, 143*, 310-312.

Sebunya, D. (2000). A study to investigate the prevalence of cryptosporidium in people frequenting the mountain gorilla (*Gorilla gorilla beringei*) habitat in Bwindi Impenetrable National Park in Southwestern Uganda. *BVM dissertation*. Kampala: Makerere University.

Sekercioglu, C. H. (2002). Effects of forestry practices on vegetation structure and bird community of Kibale National Park, Uganda. *Biological Conservation, 107*, 229-240.

Sepiria, S. R. (2000). A cross-sectional study of African Swine Fever in warthogs, giant forest hogs and Tampans of Queen Elizabeth National Park and in domestic pigs slaughtered in Kampala. *BVM Dissertation*. Kampala: Makerere University.

Serrato, A., Ibarra-Manríquez, G. and Oyama, K. (2004). Biogeography and conservation of the genus Ficus (Moraceae) in Mexico. *Journal of Biogeography, 31,* 475-485.

Shambaugh, J., Oglethorpe, J., and Ham, R. (with contributions from S. Tognetti) 2001. *The trampled grass: mitigating the impacts of armed conflict on the environment*. Biodiversity Support Program, Washington D.C.

Sheil, D., and Salim, A. (2004). Forest tree persistence, elephants, and stem scars. *Biotropica, 36,* 505-521.

Sheppard, D.J. 2000. Ecology of the Budongo Forest redtail: patterns of habitat use and population density in primary and regenerating forest sites. *MSc. Thesis*, Calgary: University of Calgary.

Shepherd, V. E., and Chapman, C. A. (1998). Dung beetles as secondary seed dispersers: Impact on seed predation and germination. *Journal of Tropical Ecology, 14,* 199-215.

Sinbaldi, I., Brouwer, J., and Corsi, F. (2004). *Possible effects of climate change on the distribution of large mammals in sub-Saharan Africa: a Modelling Study*. International Institute for Geo-Information Science and Earth Observation. Wageningen: Wageningen University.

Skorupa, J. P., Kalina, J., Butynski, T. M., Tabor, G., and Kellogg, E. (1984). Notes on the breeding biology of Cassin's hawk eagle; *Hieraaetus africanus. Ibis, 127*, 120-122.

Skorupa, J. P., and Kasenene J. M. (1984). Tropical forest management: can rates of natural treefalls help guide us? *Oryx 18*, 96-101.

Skorupa, J. P. (1986). Responses of rainforest primates to selective logging in Kibale Forest, Uganda: A summary report. In K. Benirschke (Ed.), *Primates:*

The Road to Self-sustaining Populations (Pp. 57-70). New York: Springer-Verlag.

Ssemmanda, R. (2004). A research project of the habitat preference and distribution of the handsome francolin (*Pternistis nobilis*) in the Bwindi Impenetrable National Park. *BSc dissertation*. Kampala: Makerere University.

Stewart, K. (1997). Bwindi Impenetrable National Park. *Gorilla Conservation News 11*, 2.

Stickler, C. M. (2004). The effects of selective logging on primate-habitat. interactions: a case study of redtail monkeys (*Cercopithecus ascanius*) in Kibale National Park, Uganda. *MSc. Thesis*. Florida: University of Florida, Gainesville.

Struhsaker, T. T. (1977). Infanticide and social organization in the redtail monkey (*Cercopithecus ascanius schmidti*) in the Kibale Forest, Uganda. *Zeitschrift fur Tierpsychologie, 45*, 75-84.

Struhsaker, T. T. (1978). Food habits of five monkey species in Kibale Forest, Uganda. In D. J. Chivers and J. Herbert (Eds.). *Recent Advances in Primatology*. Vol 1 Behaviour (Pp. 225-248). London: Academic Press.

Struhsaker, T. T. (1980). Comparison of the behaviour and ecology of red colobus and redtail monkeys in the Kibale Forest, Uganda. *African Journal of Ecology, 18*, 33-51.

Struhsaker, T. T. (1981a). Forest and primate conservation in East Africa. *African Journal of Ecology, 19*, 99-114.

Struhsaker, T. T. (1981b). Polyspecific associations among tropical rainforest primates. *Zeitschrift fur Tierpsychologie 57*, 268-304.

Struhsaker, T. T. (1987). Forestry issues and conservation in Uganda. *Biological Conservation, 39*, 209-234.

Struhsaker, T. T., Kasenene, J. M., Gaither, J. C. Jr, Larsen, N., Musango, S., and Bancroft, R. (1989). Tree mortality in the Kibale Forest, Uganda: A case study of dieback in a tropical rainforest adjacent to exotic conifer plantations. *Forest Ecology and Management, 29*, 165-185.

Struhsaker, T. T., Lwanga, J. S., and Kasenene, J. M. (1996). Elephants, selective logging, and forest regeneration in the Kibale Forest, Uganda. *Journal of Tropical Ecology, 12*, 45-64.

Struhsaker, T. T. 1997. *Ecology of an African rainforest: logging in Kibale and the conflict between conservation and exploitation*. Florida: University Press of Florida.

Struhsaker, T. T., and Leakey, M. (1990). Prey selectivity by crowned hawk-eagles on monkeys in the Kibale Forest, Uganda. *Behavioral Ecology and Sociobiology, 26*, 435-443.

Struhsaker, T. T. (2008). Long-term research and conservation in Kibale National Park. In R. Wrangham, and E. Ross, (Eds). *Science and Conservation in African Forests* (Pp. 27-37). Cambridge: Cambridge University Press.

Teleen, S. (1994). Group size and group structure of guereza, *Colobus guereza occidentalis* (Rochebrune 1886), in the Kibale Forest, Uganda. *Diploma*, Technischen Universitat Braunschweig.

Thompson, M. E., Wrangham, R. W., and Reynolds, V. (2006). Urinary estrone conjugates and reproductive parameters in Kibale (Kanyawara) and Budongo (Sonso) chimpanzees. In N. E. Newton-Fisher, H. Notman, J. D. Paterson, and V. Reynolds Pages, *Primates of Western Uganda* (Pp. 227-245). New York: Springer.

Tweheyo, M., and Lye, K. A. (2003). Phenology of figs in Budongo Forest, Uganda and its importance in chimpanzee diet. *African Journal of Ecology, 41,* 306-316.

Tweheyo, M., Hill, C. M., and Obua, J. (2005). Patterns of crop raiding by primates around the Budongo Forest Reserve, Uganda. *Wildlife Biology, 11,* 237-247.

Tweheyo, M., Reynolds, V., Huffman, M. A., Pebsworth, P., Goto, S., Mahaney, W. C., Milner, M. W., Waddell, A., Dirzowsky, R., and Hancock, R.G.V. (2006). Geophagy in Chimpanzees (*Pan troglodytes schweinfurthii*) of the Budongo Forest Reserve, Uganda: A multidisciplinary Study. In N. E. Newton-Fisher, H. Notman, J. D. Paterson, and V. Reynolds (Eds.) *Primates of Western Uganda* (Pp. 135-152). New York: Springer.

Twinomugisha, D., Basuta, G. I., and Chapman, C. A. (2003). Status and ecology of the golden monkey (*Cercopithecus mitis kandti*) in Mgahinga Gorilla National Park, Uganda. *African Journal of Ecology, 41,* 47-55.

Twinomugisha, D. (2007). Conservation status and determinants of golden monkey (*Cercopithecus mitis kandti*) abundance in Mgahinga Gorilla National Park. *Ph.D. Thesis.* Kampala: Makerere University.

Twinomugisha, D., C.A. Chapman, and A. Plumptre 2006. *Forest Primates.* Kampala: Uganda Biodiversity Data Bank, Makerere University Institute of Environment and Natural Resources.

UBOS (Uganda Bureau of Statistics) (2001). *Uganda National Household Survey 1999/2000.* Report on the socio-economic survey.

UWA (1996). *Semliki National Park Management Plan.* Kampala: Uganda Wildlife Authority.

UWA (2000a). *Wildlife Protected Areas System Plan for Uganda*, vol. 4: Detailed proposals for protected area changes. European Union Wildlife Support Project.

UWA (2000b). *Mt Elgon National Park General Management Plan.* Kampala: Uganda Wildlife Authority.

UWA (2001). *Bwindi Impenetrable National Park and Mgahinga Gorilla National Park General Management Plan: July 2001-June 2011.* Kampala: Uganda Wildlife Authority.

UWA (2004). *Rwenzori Mountains National Park General Management Plan 2004-2014.* Kampala: Uganda Wildlife Authority.

UWA (2005). *Semliki National Park General management plan (2005-2015).* Kampala: Uganda Wildife Authority.

U.S. Congr. Off. Technol. Assess. (1993). *Harmful non-indigenous species of the United States.* OTF-F-565. Washington D.C. van Orsdol, K. G. (1986). Agricultural encroachment in Uganda's Kibale Forest. *Oryx, 20,* 115-117.

Vitousek, P. M., D'Antonio, C. M., Loope, L. L., Rejmanek, M., and Westbrooks, R. (1997). Introduced species: a significant component of human-caused global change. *New Zealand Journal of Ecology, 21,* 1-16.

Vonesh, J. R. (2001). Patterns of richness and abundance in a tropical African leaf-litter herpetofauna. *Biotropica, 33,* 502-510.

Wagner, T. (2000). Influence of forest type and tree species on canopy-dwelling beetles in Budongo forest, Uganda. *Biotropica, 32,* 502-514.

Wanyama, F. (2005). *Ground census of mammals in Kibale National Park, Uganda.* Kampala: Uganda Wildlife Aauthority Research and Monitoring Unit.

Waser, P. M (1977a). Figs, wasps, and primates. *Africana, 6,* 23-25.

Waser, P. M. (1977b). Feeding, ranging, and group size in the mangabey *Cercocebus albigena.* In T. Clutton-Brock (Ed.). *Primate Ecology: Studies of Feeding and Ranging Behavior in Lemurs, Monkeys, and Apes* (Pp. 183-222). New York: Academic Press.

Waser, P.M. 1980. Polyspecific associations of *Cercocebus albigena*: geographic variation and ecological correlates. *Folia Primatologica, 33,* 57-76.

Waser, P. M. (1984). "Chance" and mixed species associations. *Behavioral Ecology and Sociobiology,* 15, 197-202.

Wasserman, M. D., and Chapman, C. A. (2003). Determinants of colobine monkey abundance: the importance of food energy, protein and fibre content. *Journal of Animal Ecology, 72,* 650-659.

Waterman, P. G., Mbi, C. N., McKey, D. B., and Gartlan, J. S. (1980). African rainforest vegetation and rumen microbes: phenolic compounds and nutrients as correlates of digestibility. *Oecologia (Berl.), 47,* 22-33.

Watts D., and Mitani, J. (2000). Infanticide and cannibalism by male chimpanzees at Ngogo, Kibale National Park, Uganda. *Primates, 41,* 357-365.

Watts D., and Mitani, J. (2001). Boundary patrols and intergroup encounters in wild chimpanzees. *Behaviour, 138*, 299-327.

Watts, D. (2004). Intracommunity Coalitionary Killing of an Adult Male Chimpanzee at Ngogo, Kibale National Park, Uganda. *International Journal of Primatology, 25,* 507-521.

Watts, D., Muller, M., Amsler, S. J., Mbabazi, G., and Mitani, J. C. (2006). Lethal integroup aggression by Kibale chimpanzees in Kibale National Park, Uganda. *American Journal of Primatology, 68*, 161-180.

Webster, G., and Osmaston, H. A. (2003). *A history of the Uganda Forest Department, 1951-1965.* London: Commonwealth Secretariat.

Werikhe, S. E. W. (1991). An Ecological Survey of the Gorilla Game Reserve (GGR), South-West Uganda. *MSc. Thesis.* Kampala: Makerere University.

Werikhe, S. E. W., Mushenzi, N., and Bizimana, J. (1997). *The impact of war on protected areas in central Africa.* Case study of Virunga Volcanoes region.

Webster, G. and H. A. Osmaston (2003). *A history of the Uganda Forest Department, 1951-1965.* London: Commonwealth Secretariat.

Weisenseel, K., Chapman, C. A., and Chapman, L. J. (1993). Nocturnal primates of Kibale forest: Effects of selective logging on prosimian densities. *Primates, 34*, 445-450.

Wild, R. G., and Mutebi, J. (1996). Conservation through community use of plant resources: establishing collaborative management in Bwindi Impenetrable and Mgahinga Gorilla National Park, Uganda. *People and plants working paper 5.*

Wildman, D. E., Uddin, M., Liu, G., Grossman, L. I., and Goodman, M. (2003). Implications of natural selection in shaping 99.4% nonsynonymous DNA identity between humans and chimpanzees: Enlarging genus Homo. *Proceedings of the National Academy of Sciences, 100*, 7181-7188.

Wallis J. (1997). A survey of reproductive parameters in the free-ranging chimpanzees of Gombe National Park. *Journal of Reproduction and Fertility, 109*, 297–307.

Williamson, M. (1996). *Biological Invasions.* London: Chapman and Hall.

Wimmer, R., Kirsch, S., Rappold, G. A., Schempp, W. (2002). Direct evidence for the Homo-Pan clade. *Chromosome Research, 10,* 55-61.

Wing, L. D., and I. O. Buss (1970). Elephants and forests. *Wildlife Monographs* 19.

Wrangham, R. W., and P. G. Waterman (1983). Condensed tannins in fruits eaten by chimpanzees in Gombe National Park, Tanzania. *Biotropica, 15*, 217-222.

Wrangham, R. W., and Goodall, J. (1989). Chimpanzee use of medicinal leaves. In P. Heltne and L. Marquardt (Eds.) *Understanding Chimpanzees* (Pp. 22-37). Cambridge: Harvard University Press.

Wrangham, R. W., Conklin, N. L., Chapman, C. A., and Hunt, K. D. (1991). The significance of fibrous foods for the Kibale forest chimpanzees. *Philosophical Transanctions of the Royal Society of London B, 334*, 171-178.

Wrangham, R. W., Rogers, M. E., and Basuta, G. I. (1993). Ape food density in the ground layer in Kibale Forest, Uganda. *African Journal of Ecology, 31*, 49-57.

Wrangham, R. W., de Wall, F. B. M., and McGrew, W. C. (1994a). *The challenge of behavioral diversity.* In R. W. Wrangham, W. C. McGrew, F. B. M. de Waal, and P.G. Heltne (Eds.). *Chimpanzee Cultures.* Cambridge Massachusetts: Harvard University Press.

Wrangham, R. W., Chapman, C. A., and Chapman, L. J. (1994b). Seed dispersal by forest chimpanzees in Uganda. *Journal of Tropical Ecology*, 10, 355-368.

Wrangham, R. W. (1995). Relationship of chimpanzee leaf swallowing to a tapeworm infection. *American Journal of Primatology, 37*, 297-303.

Wrangham, R. W., and Peterson, D. (1996). *Demonic Males: Apes and the Origins of Human Violence.* Boston: Houghton Mifflin.

Wrangham, R. W. (2000). Kibale Snare Removal Program 1997-2000: *Interim report to the Jane Goodall Institute*, Uganda Wildlife Education Centre.

Wrangham, R. W., and Mugume, S. (2000). Snare removal program in Kibale National Park: a preliminary report. *Pan Africa News, 7*, 18-20.

Wrangham, R. W. 2001. Moral decisions about wild chimpanzees. In B. B. Beck, T. S. Stoinski, M. Hutchins, T. L. Maple, B. Norton, A. Rowan, E. F. Stevens, and A. Arluke (Eds) *Great Apes and Humans: The Ethics of Coexistence*, (Pp. 230-244). Washington: Smithsonian Institute.

Wrangham, R. W. (2008). Why the link between long-term research and conservation is a case worth making. In R. Wrangham and E. Ross, (Eds). *Science and Conservation in African Forests* (Pp 1-8). Cambridge: Cambridge University Press.

Yatuha, J. (2004). The breeding ecology of the Stripe-breasted tit in Bwindi Impenetrable National Park, Southwestern Uganda. *MSc. Thesis.* Kampala: Makerere University.

Zanne, A. E. (1998). Expediting indigenous tree regeneration in degraded frasslands: plantations and the effects of distance and isolation from seed sources. *MSc. Thesis.* Gainesville: University of Florida.

Zanne, A. E., and Chapman, C. A. (2001). Expediting reforestation in tropical grasslands: distance and isolation from seed sources in plantations. *Ecological Applications, 11*, 1610-1621.

Zanne, A., Keith, B., Chapman, C. A., and Chapman, L. J. (2001). Protecting terrestrial mammal communities: potential role of pine plantations. *African Journal of Ecology, 39*, 399-401.

INDEX

A

accessibility, 12
accounting, 74
accuracy, 69
acid, 27, 28, 51
acute, 2, 78, 89
Adams, 77, 131
adjustment, 49
administration, 3, 9, 14, 18, 88
administrators, 18
adolescents, 53
adsorption, 49
adult, 44, 45, 46, 47, 52, 58, 74, 76
adulthood, 97
Africa, xv, 2, 6, 16, 17, 21, 22, 25, 28, 30, 31, 35, 55, 58, 116, 133, 135, 136, 144, 150, 151, 154, 155
African continent, 13
age, 18, 22, 44, 58, 132
agents, 71, 78, 119, 135
aggression, 45, 154
aging, 82
agricultural, ix, x, 21, 30, 62, 63, 83, 86, 87, 88, 89, 103, 120, 138
agricultural crop, x
agriculture, 11, 12, 36, 69, 106, 109, 136
aiding, 95, 112
air, 62, 133
algae, 103

alkaline, 34
allies, 28
alluvial, 34
alternative, 47
alternative energy, 47
alternatives, 109, 135
alters, 96
amphibia, 30
amphibians, 25, 102
Angola, 32
animal health, 78
annual rate, 65
antagonists, 95
antibiotic, 49
application, 142
applied research, vii, 3, 129
aquatic systems, 61, 126
armed conflict, 95, 150
arthropod, 77, 103
arthropods, 73, 102, 103
ash, 61
assessment, 9, 65, 69, 106, 108, 109, 122, 136
attacks, 14, 45, 52, 53, 113
attitudes, 106, 107, 108, 111, 112, 122
Australia, 62, 64, 78
authority, 107
availability, 71, 72, 74, 75, 90, 102, 111, 133, 134, 135, 136, 144
averaging, 45, 46
avoidance, 93

I

N

O

P

S

swallowing, 49, 155
swamps, 25, 26, 36, 54, 61
Switzerland, 139
symptoms, 77
synergistic effect, 134

T

tall trees, 86
tannin, 47, 74
tannins, 47, 61, 148, 154
Tanzania, 154
tapeworm, 155
taxa, x, 24, 68, 103
taxonomic, 84, 149
tea, 8, 62, 94, 123
telephone, 8
temperate zone, 60
temperature, 22, 28, 34, 73, 75, 103, 126
temporal, 133
tenure, 12
termites, 50
terraces, 14
territory, 45
thinking, vii, 1, 35
threat, 90, 146
threatened, 2, 23, 24, 25, 32, 35, 70, 94
threats, ix, xv, 13, 41, 78, 107, 117, 135
threshold, 81
threshold level, 81
timber, 2, 3, 8, 10, 12, 13, 18, 19, 20, 38, 41,
    59, 82, 83, 90, 103, 104, 106, 115, 116,
    119, 120, 126, 144, 147
time periods, 74, 134
tin, 20
tobacco, 8
tolerance, 104
topsoil, 97
total product, 56
tourism, 10, 12, 16, 17, 42, 87, 95, 105, 107,
    109, 110, 115, 116, 119, 122, 143
tourist, 77, 110, 119
toxic, 49
toxins, 49, 51, 104, 121, 145
tracking, 149

tradition, x, 18
trans, 5
transfer, 45, 145, 146
transition, 22
transmission, 8, 77, 78, 110, 116
transparency, 103
traps, 78, 91, 112, 113
travel, 42, 58, 100, 110
tree cover, 17, 18, 47, 82, 83, 120
tribes, 14
tropical forest, ix, x, 4, 12, 84, 125, 133, 134,
    135, 136, 144, 147
tropical forests, x, 12, 125, 144, 147
tropical rain forests, 52, 136
trust, 107
trust fund, 107
tubers, 109
tuff, 35

U

UNESCO, xiv, 18, 116
uniform, ix
United Kingdom, 139
United Nations, xiv
United States, 94, 153
USAID, 141, 146

V

vacuum, 20
values, 2, 9, 32, 50
variability, 25, 79
variables, 69
variation, ix, 21, 31, 73, 74, 81, 120, 132, 133,
    134, 145, 146, 153
vegetation, 2, 12, 22, 23, 26, 27, 29, 30, 32,
    33, 34, 36, 37, 38, 39, 47, 51, 54, 55, 61,
    63, 65, 92, 93, 96, 98, 99, 103, 104, 106,
    110, 117, 150, 153
vertebrates, 25, 77, 138
victims, 50
Victoria, 8, 35, 36
village, 92, 113, 116